Prai

Flying, Fall

"I am very grateful for Carolyn Whitney-Brown's accurate account of my brother Henri's inner feelings, hopes, wishes, and despair. You brought Henri very close to me again."

—Laurent Nouwen, founder of the Henri Nouwen Foundation

"In Carolyn Whitney-Brown's deft hands, Henri's intentions literally, vividly swing alive. This is a beautiful, moving story about inter-connectivity, interdependence, and life's rich, beautiful, complicated pageant. I devoured it in a sitting."

—Lisa Napoli, author of *Ray & Joan: The Man Who Made the McDonald's Fortune and the Woman Who Gave It All Away*

"A loving achievement and a riveting story of spirit meets body. With splendid pace and wit, Carolyn Whitney-Brown drops the words of Henri Nouwen's flights of thought before us. Then, she arranges to gorgeously catch them. A singular spiritual tale written with tender-hearted eloquence from two arresting minds."

—Kathryn Bond Stockton, author of *Gender(s)* and Distinguished Professor of English at the University of Utah

"A lifelong search for wholeness takes a surprising late turn—toward the circus! As someone who's spent much of my adult life absorbing beautiful spiritual truths in gritty entertainment venues, I can defi-nitely relate."

—Shad, rapper and host of the documentary series *Hip-Hop Evolution*

"Anyone who knew Henri, either through his writing or in person, will immediately recognize how beautifully he's been brought to life in this book—his willingness to write so vulnerably about human relationships and feelings as a means to discovering our purpose in life, and a sense of the divine."

—Gary Donohoe, professor of psychology at University of Galway

"*Flying, Falling, Catching* is far beyond religious belief or affiliation. It is a universal tale of mind-body connection and disconnection. While undoubtedly an account of a spiritual journey, Carolyn Whitney-Brown nimbly explores the corporeal inner life of Henri Nouwen as he literally swings through the air. It is brilliant!"

—Ruth Rakoff, author of *When My World Was Very Small*

"*Flying, Falling, Catching* is a beacon of hope. It reminds us that despite all the perils and sufferings that surround us, with which we often collide, we can find healing, peace, and awe even in the most unusual detours that life offers. A must read."

—Marina Nemat, author of *Prisoner of Tehran*

"To fly, to fall, and be caught again. It is everything a beloved community hopes to be."

—*The Banner* magazine (Christian Reformed Church in North America)

"A theologically inflected narrative that explores Nouwen's fascination with a group of trapeze artists while imagining what he experienced during the last days of his life. Whitney-Brown's story circles around

[Nouwen's] unfinished manuscript and its recurring themes of vulnerability, trust, fear, bravery, and freedom."

—*The Christian Century*

"Highly readable and compelling, the author weaves together Nouwen's writings and her own narrative style into a thoughtful and engaging story that will resonate with anyone interested in the big questions about friendship, fear, and how we show up for each other."

—Goodreads

"No question that flying, falling, and catching were unlikely teachers for Henri Nouwen, whose clear preferences were security, stability, and being caught. I hope and trust that you, the reader, will allow Henri to guide your journey through risk to freedom!"

—Sister Sue Mosteller, CSJ, executrix of Henri Nouwen's
    literary estate

"In this book, I see Henri in the audience, smiling straight at me, clapping his hands above his head, enjoying our performance success as much as we did. This one is for you, my friend."

—Rodleigh Stevens, founder of the Flying Rodleighs and
    former trainer with Cirque du Soleil

"For Henri Nouwen, a flying trapeze performance was like a Russian icon, drawing him into a spiritual world. This endearing true story about living and dying carefully brings together all of Nouwen's thinking on the Flying Rodleighs and the circus. Like the act itself, sheer elegance."

—Michael Ford, author of *Wounded Prophet* and *Lonely Mystic*

"This is a book full of insight. . . . In this ostensibly non-religious circus troupe, Nouwen discerned 'a community of love that can break through the boundaries of ordinariness.' Whitney-Brown captures with wit and tenderness the 'odd-couple' friendship between the gawky writer-priest and the circus artistes. . . . Ultimately, insights abound. Nouwen's notebooks reveal how the Rodleighs deepen his understanding of human difference and otherness, and inspire him to fresh insights into the nature of vocation."

—*Church Times* (UK)

"A beautiful example of how even the most exquisite of truths are revealed to us through imperfect people and inauspicious circumstances."

—*Quill & Quire* (Canada)

"A fascinating read, both as a portrait of Nouwen and for the insight it offers into his creative process."

—*Broadview Magazine* (Canada)

"An intriguing capper to one of the best known thinkers of religion since Thomas Merton."

—Broadway Direct's "The Best New Theater Books for This Spring 2022"

"Whitney-Brown beautifully captures Nouwen as a joy-filled, almost child-like spiritual risk-taker who found a freedom in his later years as his carefully structured life increasingly became one of unpredictability, learning, vulnerability, and even failures."

—Richard Propes

FLYING
FALLING
CATCHING

An Unlikely Story of Finding Freedom

Henri J. M. Nouwen

and

Carolyn Whitney-Brown

HarperOne
An Imprint of HarperCollinsPublishers

To Geoffrey Whitney-Brown
because no one flies alone

For Sister Sue Mosteller, CSJ, beloved friend of Henri Nouwen,
a ground-breaking flyer in her own right
and the one who kept this story alive

HarperCollins books may be purchased for educational, business, or sales promotional use. For information, please email the Special Markets Department at SPsales@harpercollins.com.

FIRST HARPERCOLLINS PAPERBACK PUBLISHED IN 2024

Designed by Joy O'Meara @ Creative Joy Designs

Illustrations: © Shutterstock (modified by The Book Designers)

Library of Congress Cataloging-in-Publication Data is available upon request.

ISBN 978-0-06-311353-4

24 25 26 27 28 LBC 5 4 3 2 1

When I saw the Flying Rodleighs for the very first time, it looked like everything that's important in life. I saw it together in one act.

—HENRI NOUWEN

The ten minutes that followed somehow gave me a glimpse of a world that had eluded me so far, a world of discipline and freedom, diversity and harmony, risk and safety, individuality and community, and most of all flying and catching.

—HENRI NOUWEN

CONTENTS

Prologue: September 1996 1

I
The Call 7

II
Falling 39

III
Teamwork 93

IV
Trust the Catcher 125

V
Flying 181

Epilogue 227

ACKNOWLEDGMENTS 231

NOTES 235

CREDITS AND PERMISSIONS 261

PROLOGUE

September 1996

When they received the phone call telling them of Henri's death, the five members of the Flying Rodleighs trapeze troupe were stunned. Before removing their flashy silver capes during their next performance, Rodleigh Stevens took a deep breath and offered a short speech dedicating the performance to the memory of their friend Henri Nouwen.

On the day of Henri's funeral, Rodleigh with his wife and colleague Jennie Stevens drove 170 miles to St. Catherine's Cathedral in Utrecht. They looked up into the stone Gothic arches and around the enormous space, amazed that it was so full.

"We should have expected this," Rodleigh whispered to Jennie. They knew that Henri was famous, with millions of books in print, translated into dozens of languages. They knew that Henri was a Roman Catholic priest from the Netherlands who had been a professor at Yale and Harvard, then over the past decade had given up his

PROLOGUE

academic career to live with people with intellectual disabilities in
Canada.

They had known Henri well for more than five years, but they
were shocked when one speaker described Henri as "anguished" and
"wounded." Rodleigh shifted uneasily and clutched the edge of the
hard wooden pew to hold himself back from rushing to the front of
the church to offer a corrective. His mind was full of images and
memories of the very different Henri that he knew through visits,
letters, and traveling together in Germany and the Netherlands with
the Circus Barum.

PERHAPS MANY OF HENRI's friends, aware of his yearning and inner
pain, and many who for years read his personally revealing books on
the spiritual life, would have been equally surprised to discover that
Henri believed his most important book was going to be a work of
creative nonfiction about his experiences with the Flying Rodleighs,
a book that his sudden death in September 1996 left unfinished.

•••••

THE STORY YOU WILL read here is true. Every event actually happened,
including Henri's rescue out a hotel window. Texts in italics are Henri's
own words from his published or unpublished writings, talks or interviews.

Though Henri found acclaim and success writing books of spiritual wisdom, the Flying Rodleighs inspired him to imagine writing a
different kind of book. When he died suddenly in 1996, he left hints
of this new project: a transcript from his dictation immediately after

meeting these trapeze artists for the first time in 1991, two chapters composed later, a journal written while traveling with the Flying Rodleighs, and other comments, reflections, notes, and journal entries.

In 2017, the publishing committee of the Henri Nouwen Legacy Trust approached me to "do something creative" with Henri's unpublished trapeze writings. I was a writer who knew Henri well. After completing my PhD in English literature at Brown University and training as a spiritual director in the United Kingdom and Canada, I lived at L'Arche Daybreak with my husband and children from 1990 to 1997, where Henri was also a community member. Shortly after Henri's death, I wrote an introduction to a new edition of his book *The Road to Daybreak*, as well as several other published pieces about him. Still, I was unsure about taking up Henri's unfinished project. I remembered many conversations with Henri about writing and about the Flying Rodleighs, but the trapeze imagery had never grabbed my imagination. I don't like heights.

When I read Henri's material, however, two questions intrigued me. First, why did the Flying Rodleighs' performance and lives strike Henri so powerfully at that moment in his life? Second, why didn't he write more than some fragments of a trapeze book? He wrote a lot of books between 1991 and 1996, and he talked continually about his desire to write this one. What happened?

I realized that my project was not to write the book that Henri would have written, but to tell the story of Henri and the Flying Rodleighs.

Combing through Henri's trapeze notes and drafts as well as Henri's other published and unpublished writing, I began to sense an overarching shape in his life's last few years. Four kinds of experiences stood out: Henri's reflections on artistry and beauty; times when his physical response helped him to articulate how *the body tells a spiritual story*; transformative points of immersion in specific communities; and moments of lightness, humor, relaxation, and delight.

Ideas for how I might bring Henri's experiences to the page began to form, but it took reading Rodleigh Stevens's memoir of his friendship with Henri, titled "What a Friend We Had in Henri," to give me details for a book that would read as engagingly as fiction while using true events. Rodleigh's memoir also helped clarify something that had been niggling at me: while Henri was often anguished and demanding, he was also delightful. Reading Rodleigh's account, at points I laughed out loud remembering our eager, awkward, insightful friend. There is a reason his friends still miss him all these years later.

Henri had envisioned writing this story as a work of "creative nonfiction." All of Henri's writing is creative, of course. His artistry is apparent even in his published journals, as Henri crafted himself into a character in his own narrative, selecting the details that he wished to share.

Even allowing for Henri's desire to tell a "creative" story, I needed to understand what actually happened the day of Henri's first heart attack. How is a patient in the midst of a medical emergency taken out a window? Dennie Wulterkens, a specialist who trained nurses to do this kind of rescue in the 1990s, responded to my email and explained the process in detail. Because we have been unable to identify the historic person who responded to the call, I have named the character of the nurse "Dennie" in thanks. Even in a medical crisis, Henri would have tried to learn the name of the person caring for him.

Except for "Dennie," all characters are real people, with their own names. My main artistic license is to imagine that during his heart attack in the Netherlands on September 16, 1996, Henri reflects back over parts of his life. This is not a biography. Many important people and experiences in Henri's life are not included.

Because I want you to hear Henri's voice as directly as possible, his writings are italicized and never rewritten. Occasionally I abbreviated or factually corrected them. Sources are provided in detailed notes at the end of the book.

"I wasn't thinking of using the Rodleighs as illustrations for great spiritual truths, but was simply trying to write a good story," Henri once told his German editor. I believe this is, as Henri hoped, a very good story. Along the way, you may also catch some unexpected insights. I know I did.

But first, jump in and enjoy the story!

Carolyn Whitney-Brown
Cowichan Bay, BC, Canada
September 16, 2021

I

The Call

1

Two paramedics in crisp white uniforms burst into Henri's hotel room. They are speaking rapidly in Dutch, his mother tongue. Henri, lying on the hotel bed still in his travel clothes, is relieved to see them.

One introduces himself as Dennie, and reaches out to shake Henri's hand. Henri's eyes behind his glasses are bright, but Dennie observes that his handshake is unsteady and his skin is cool. Dennie explains to Henri that he is a registered nurse with the Broeder De Vries ambulance service.

The other introduces himself as the ambulance driver, also a trained paramedic. He looks around the pleasant room, quickly assessing what Henri has with him in case he needs to go to the hospital. Henri has not unpacked any of his luggage.

Dennie shines his flashlight into Henri's eyes to check his pupils. He takes Henri's pulse and slips his arm into a blood-pressure cuff, all the while asking Henri questions: "What is your name? Where are you from?"

Henri is tired and feels dizzy, but answers as clearly as he can: he is Father Henri J. M. Nouwen. He arrived in Amsterdam at Schiphol airport that morning on an overnight flight from Toronto, Canada, and came straight to the hotel to rest.

"Do you know the date today, and where you are right now?"

"Yes," says Henri. It is Monday, September 16, 1996. He is in Hilversum, at the Hotel Lapershoek. He knows that he is on an upper floor, though he cannot remember his room number.

"What is your main complaint? Do you have any other complaints?"

"My chest hurts a lot. My arm is sore. I am hot and cold."

"When did it start? Have you ever had something like this before?"

"No," says Henri. "I wasn't feeling well yesterday, but I figured it was not serious, and I could rest as soon as I arrived. But it has been getting worse since I checked into the hotel a little over an hour ago."

Dennie evaluates Henri's blood pressure. Henri is glad the questions have paused. His mind is whirling with words and images, but speaking is too much effort.

This is, Henri thinks to himself, an interruption. He has mixed feelings. There have been many interruptions in his life. Some of them have turned out well.

·····•

FIVE YEARS EARLIER, HENRI was in Freiburg, Germany, working on a book when he first saw the Flying Rodleighs perform their trapeze act. It left him breathless, almost in tears as a sudden bodily rush of adolescent infatuation swept over him. He was already fifty-nine years old, so he had not expected to be so stirred when he went to the circus with his elderly father. At first, he had assumed that his sensations were anxiety, because the act looked dangerous. It was only later that he recognized his own physical excitement. His response had been so dramatic that he repeatedly struggled to put words around it. First he had tried dictating a tape to be transcribed by Connie, his secretary back in Canada. He knew he was babbling, but he couldn't help himself.

What really got to me, what really fascinated me was the trapeze artists, and that's why I became so involved in the circus and, when I saw them at the very beginning it was absolutely fascinating. This was a group of five trapeze artists, four of them people from South Africa and one an American. I was just so impressed by this group that I kept thinking about them. They did incredible things in the air and somehow, and that was important that I realized that, that has always been why I went to the circus. It was never for the animals and never really for the clowns, but what I was always waiting for and what really grabbed me was the trapeze artists.

And these guys were really amazing. Actually, they weren't all guys; there were three men and two women, and I was just fascinated by the way they were moving freely in the air and making these incredible jumps, and catching each other, and I was just fascinated by their physical prowess.

But I was as much fascinated by the group as a team, the way they worked together because I realized there must be enormous intimacy among these people when everything is so dependent on co-operation, when everything is so dependent on mutual trust and everything is dependent on exact timing.

I realized from the very beginning that this group has to be really well together, and I saw that they enjoyed it, they really had fun doing it, and there was a kind of excitement in them that became very contagious for me.

It was kind of a WOW! you know, and I must confess that when I saw them they seemed to be in a way like gods, so far that I wouldn't even dare to come close to them. I had this emotional response that these people are really so far above me in their talent or in their giftedness. They are such great artists, who am I, a little tiny guy wanting to get to know them. It seemed to be impossible for me to even imagine myself knowing these people personally. I realized how strong that feeling was. It was like awesome, awesome, and there was something in me more than just a feeling of a fan who admires a musician or artist. It was as if these guys are indeed living in heaven; they are living in the air and I am living on the ground, and so I am not allowed to talk to them, being so far from each other.

I was so fascinated by my own emotional response to them that I wasn't at all comfortable to go and talk to them. They kept sort of being in my fantasies long after the show was over.

So I went to the show and saw it again, and I began, you know, watching all the other acts, but as soon as these Flying Rodleighs came on, I got all excited again. The whole way they walked right in there and they climbed up to the top of the tent and made these enormous jumps, and the music and their whole style, their smiling at each other, and the fun they had, and their timing, and the whole thing. I couldn't believe they were doing it. The second time I was even more fascinated than the first. It was just unbelievable and I got very nervous inside because I thought I am going to talk to these guys when this is over. It is like talking to people from another planet.

Henri could not get this experience out of his mind. Perhaps this unlikely new encounter with a troupe of trapeze artists wasn't an interruption from his writing, but rather was the start of a significant new book. Surely he could find a way to describe this experience. Something this amazing should be shared. It was all very exhilarating.

·····•

BUT NOW IT IS 1996 and he is lying on a hotel bed near Amsterdam with two paramedics hovering around him. Somehow five years have gone by since that trip to the circus with his father. It has never been far from his mind, yet he has only fragments of chapters, a diary kept over several weeks, and many ideas. He has failed, at least so far, to write his book about the Flying Rodleighs.

What would it feel like to let go, he wonders now, watching Dennie get out his medical equipment.

I never did write that book, he tries whispering to himself. It feels strange to admit that, as though it is a finished fact, as though he could have but didn't. A casual comment, small talk. Unless, of course, an astute listener were to ask, "Why?"

To that, he realizes, he does not have an answer.

2

Dennie unbuttons Henri's shirt and moves his undershirt aside to listen to his heart. The room isn't especially cold but Henri isn't accustomed to being bare-chested, especially in front of an audience. He shivers.

·····

A FEW MONTHS AFTER meeting the Flying Rodleighs, Henri reread the typed text of his dictated words about the trapeze troupe and smiled. He loved remembering those magical days. He ran his fingers through his thinning hair and thought about the text. It didn't catch quite what he wanted to say. Or perhaps more accurately, this wasn't how he wanted to say it. He didn't want merely to describe his excitement, he wanted the reader to feel the same way. He sighed with frustration. He wanted to tell a story, a story of infatuation, even of falling in love with the Flying Rodleighs. But although he was a prolific writer, he had never attempted a *story*.

Always eager to learn, he bought two books about writing. Passages in Theodore Cheney's *Writing Creative Nonfiction* seemed to catch what he longed to do. *Use concrete details,* he wrote in the margin. "Develop the story scene by scene," he underlined.

He tried again, setting a sophisticated European scene, depicting himself as a spiritual writer peacefully composing a gentle book about love and inner freedom.

Visiting the south German city of Freiburg has always been a great pleasure for me. The most peaceful and joyful memories of the last few decades are from that city so beautifully situated between the river Rhine and the edge of the Black Forest.

In April 1991, I was there again for another month of writing. The L'Arche Daybreak community in Toronto, where I have found my home since 1986, encourages me to take at least two months a year away from the intense and busy life with mentally handicapped people and to "indulge" myself guilt-free in collecting thoughts, ideas and stories to articulate new visions about the ways in which God's Spirit makes its healing presence known among us.

I love Daybreak: the people, the work, the festivities, but I also realize that they can so completely absorb all my time and energy, that it is practically impossible to keep asking the question: "What is it all about anyhow?"

I spent most of my day in the guest room on the third floor of a small house of Franciscans, writing about "the life of the Beloved." Over the past years at Daybreak, the residents of Daybreak have helped me to rediscover the simple but profound truth that all people, handicapped or not, are the beloved daughters and sons of God and that they can find true inner freedom by claiming that truth for themselves.

This spiritual insight touched me so deeply that I wanted to spend a whole month thinking and writing about it in the hope that I would be able to help myself and others to overcome the deep-seated temptation of self-rejection.

"Nonfiction writers limit themselves to showing us how things really look to them in the world, leaving the reader to interpret what it all means," Henri read, and he underlined it, this time telling the story without interpretation.

However, this time in Freiburg was going to become unique. It bore a gift I could never have imagined before: the gift of a completely new image of humanity's belovedness—an image that would occupy my soul for many years. It was so surprising, so refreshing and so revealing that it would take me on a new journey, one that I could never have foreseen, not even in my wildest dreams.

Let me tell you how it came about. It all began with my father, who lives in the Netherlands and who had expressed a great interest in visiting me in Freiburg.

During the week my father and I were together, I forgot about my writing; we spent all of our time "going places," even though my father's weak heart prevented him from taking long walks. Since museums and churches were too tiring to visit, I looked for concerts or movies to entertain us. As I was going through the newspaper and asking people about interesting events to attend, someone jokingly said: "Well, the circus is in town!" The circus, the circus! I had not been to a circus for many years—I had not even thought about it since I had seen the Ringling–Barnum and Bailey Circus in New Haven, Connecticut. I said to my father: "Would you like to go to the circus?" There was little hesitation. "I'd love to go," he said. "Let's do it!"

Franz Johna, his wife, Reny, their son, Robert, my father, and I went to the circus. It was Circus Simoneit Barum, and it had just come to town. I didn't know what to expect. My main hope was that my father would enjoy it and that we all would have a good evening: hearty laughs, great surprises, pleasant conversation, and a good meal afterward. I was not at all prepared for an experience that would deeply influence my future thinking, reading, and writing.

The program was quite traditional: horses, tigers, lions, zebra, el-ephants, and even a giraffe and a rhinoceros. It all was delightful en-tertainment, but I would have forgotten the evening within a few days and gone back to my writing on "The Life of the Beloved" without any thought about the circus if there hadn't been the "Flying Rodleighs."

As the last act before the intermission, five trapeze artists, two women and three men, entered the ring as if they were queens and kings. After having greeted the audience with a movement that made their wide silver capes swirl about them, they removed them, handed them to the attendants, pulled themselves up into the large net, and started to climb the rope ladders that brought them to their positions high up in the tent. From the very moment they appeared, my atten-tion was completely riveted. The self-confident and joyful way they entered, smiled, greeted the audience, and then climbed to the trapeze rigging told me that I was going to see something—better, experience something—that was going to make this evening unlike any other.

"A scene reproduces the motion of life; life is motion, action." He liked that. What he needed to communicate about the trapeze was motion and action. His other books had been shaped by a message he wished to convey, but this book was different. He was not entirely sure what his experience meant, just that it was so powerful and physical that he wanted to share it.

> *The ten minutes that followed somehow gave me a glimpse of a world that had eluded me so far, a world of discipline and freedom, diversity and harmony, risk and safety, individuality and community, and most of all flying and catching.*
>
> *I sat transfixed in my chair and couldn't believe what I saw.*

Yes, that's it, Henri thought as he paused in his writing. Flying and catching. It's everything I have always desired.

> *I still do not know precisely what happened that evening. Was it the presence of my eighty-eight-year-old father that made me see something eternal in a trapeze act that, for many, is simply one of the entertaining events in a two-hour-long circus program? (He certainly had something to do with it, since his visit had about it that wonderful quality of mutual freedom and mutual bonding that can develop when both father and son have become elders.) Or was it my intense concentration on the call to claim my own belovedness as an eternal gift and the call to proclaim that belovedness to others without condition?*
>
> *There is little doubt that my heart and mind were very disposed to see new visions and hear new sounds. And why wouldn't the angels of God come to me in the incarnation of five trapeze artists? It also is possible that my being so far away from the ordinary duties and responsibilities in my community and the unusual opportunity of using*

time and space in such an unprescribed way opened me to a new, inner knowledge.

Sitting in the circus, I knew that I was free to see what I wanted and needed to see and that no one could force me to limit my vision to seeing simply a well-performed but never-perfect piece of aerial acrobatics.

Henri reread his paragraph. *No one could force me to limit my vision.* Why had he written that? It seemed a rather juvenile thought, as though he had to resist some judgmental outside authority that wanted to limit his perceptions or experience. But perhaps, he realized, feeling juvenile was precisely the point, because watching the Flying Rodleighs pulled him back to a much earlier moment in his life.

One thing I was certain of from the moment I saw the five artists entering the ring. They took me back forty-three years when, as a sixteen-year-old teenager, I first saw trapeze artists in a Dutch circus. I do not remember much of that event, except for the trapeze. The trapeze act gave rise to a desire in me that no other art form could evoke: the desire to belong to a community of love that can break through the boundaries of ordinariness.

Although I hadn't an athletic bone in my body and never participated to any significant degree in competitive sports, the trapeze became a dream for me. To be a trapeze artist symbolized for me the realization of the human desire for self-transcendence—rising above oneself, glimpsing the heart of things.

Sitting with my father in the Freiburg circus this teenage desire returned to my mind in full force. I had not thought about it for more than forty years, but how vivid and real it was—as if all those years had slipped by in one second. So much and so little had happened between 1948 and 1991. Perhaps all that had happened were just variations on the same desire for self-transcendence. Becoming a priest, studying psychology and theology, travelling all over the world, writing and speaking for the most varied groups of readers and listeners, leaving my country, teaching at different universities, and finally joining a community with mentally handicapped people—weren't they all attempts to be a flyer and a catcher?

As I sat there at the circus in Freiburg in April 1991, I suddenly saw my pure desire acted out in front of me and realized that what those five artists did was all I ever wanted to do.

A community of love that can break through the boundaries of ordinariness. My pure desire, repeated Henri to himself.

The Flying Rodleighs were stunning, the women in outfits that reminded him of swimsuits, and the men bare-chested in sparkling spandex tights. Henri had always been attracted to men. He had known that about himself since an early age. Among his close friends, Henri identified himself as a gay man who took his vows of celibacy as a priest seriously. But he was moved by more than the physical beauty of the Rodleighs. There was also the freedom, teamwork, and graceful community and joy between them.

Henri reread his words. *Variations on the same desire for self-transcendence.* Or maybe for escape? Or belonging? Even writing about the experience left Henri shaken with emotions he could hardly name, welling into tears. But it hadn't ended there. He pushed himself to keep writing.

A few days after that enlightening evening, my father returned to the Netherlands, and I returned to my writing project. Although Franz and Reny Johna, their son Robert and especially my father had enjoyed the circus, we didn't speak much about it anymore. Other events and other people asked our attention, and the human inclination to return to the familiar reduced the circus experience to a pleasant distraction.

However, back with the Franciscans, I overheard the superior say to one of the students: "Let's go to the circus tonight!" While I do not remember having been drawn to see the same movie more than once, the thought of going to the circus again filled me with excitement, and it wasn't hard to be invited by the superior and his students to join them. Just before leaving, I went to my room, picked up the Circus Barum program that I had bought a few days earlier, and looked up the page about the trapeze artists. There I read:

Strength and Spirit—in this presentation we meet a medical technician, a trained nurse, a teacher in athletics, a ship builder and a clown. Rod, the leader of the group, his wife Jennie, his sister Karlene and the catcher Johan Jonas all come from South Africa. Jon, the second catcher, is an American and comes from the Ringling Circus. All these talented people find themselves together in one of the best flying trapeze acts.

As I read this description of the five artists, my heart started to beat faster. It seemed as if I had been given a look behind the curtain of one of the most moving acts I had ever seen. I suddenly experienced feelings that were quite new for me: curiosity, admiration, and an intense desire to be close, but also feelings of awe, distance, and a strange sense of shyness. I don't remember ever having been an ardent fan of anyone. My room was never decorated with posters of sports heroes or music stars. But now I felt that strange mixture of worship and fear that must make up the heart of an adolescent who has fallen in love with an idol on an unreachable stage.

3

Dennie reaches under the blanket and feels Henri's feet and ankles. Somewhat swollen, he says, but that could be because he got off an overnight flight just hours earlier. He asks the driver to hand him the LifePak 10 monitor-defibrillator, and secures three EKG leads to Henri's chest.

He attaches a finger clip to Henri's right hand, explaining that it can measure the amount of oxygen in his blood. Henri is grateful that Dennie is explaining what is happening. It makes him feel safer.

"I also need to insert an IV to check your glucose levels and perhaps to give you medication," Dennie says, "and I will do that now in case your blood pressure drops and it becomes more difficult to find a vein. Are you right-handed or left-handed?"

Right-handed, responds Henri, wincing as the nurse inserts the needle in the back of his left hand.

"Can you raise your head?" Dennie asks. Henri tries, and immediately feels faint and dizzy. Suddenly the room is full of motion. Dennie looks at the monitor-defibrillator and grabs his portable radio.

Henri hears his voice, speaking urgently now, asking his dispatcher to notify the fire department with a top-priority request to assist with the rescue of a patient from an upper floor of Hotel Lapershoek. They will go to Ziekenhuis Hilversum: Could the dispatcher ensure that there will be a team waiting in the ICU for a heart patient?

Henri waits for the dizzying movement to subside. He does not feel in imminent danger, but the call sounds like an emergency.

The ambulance driver is now on the phone calling down to the front desk. Two fire trucks will be arriving, he tells the hotel manager. Can someone from maintenance come now to open the largest moving window? Yes, immediately.

Dennie puts the portable radio into its holder and turns back to Henri. He sees that Henri is struggling to make sense of what he overheard. Henri would probably appreciate a direct answer to his unspoken questions.

"This situation is a bit unusual," Dennie gently explains. "We have the ambulance waiting in the parking lot, but the elevator is too small for a stretcher. You need to stay horizontal, so there is no way to go down in the elevator. We cannot take you down the stairs, either. They are too steep and your blood pressure is low."

Henri seems to be following the explanation. Dennie takes a breath and makes sure he has eye contact with Henri because this next bit of information is the most important.

"We have called the fire department. They will take you out through a window."

Henri's eyes widen. Is he in pain, or frightened? Dennie is not sure. He doesn't seem tense. Henri looks like he would like to say something, but remains silent.

Out a window. Even in his discomfort, Henri is intrigued. Just nine months ago in Prague he wrote in his journal, *I have learned a new word:*

defenestration. It happened, he learned, in 1419 and again in 1618 when people threw their opponents out the window, and probably in 1948 as well. Henri had added lightheartedly, *I had never heard of this strange 'custom' but I have decided to keep my windows closed!*

Fortunately, the paramedics now proposing to defenestrate him seem friendly.

·····

ALL HIS LIFE, THE experience of people at the top, the high-flyers in any field, held a particular fascination for Henri. Even back in his university days, Henri's friends saw him as a social climber. But Henri did not cultivate relationships only with important people. He was interested in everyone, in every social strata. Like his father, he liked people who did things well, with artistry, with discipline, with conviction. Where did it come from, this wide-ranging curiosity, the insistent desire to experience the world from another perspective, to get inside other people's skin?

It went deeper than curiosity. Maybe it was a kind of self-rejection. All his life, Henri had wanted a different body. For as long as he could remember, his body had hungers that were never satisfied. His mother blamed the strict instructions she had been given when he was an infant, to feed him only every four hours no matter how hungry and desperate he was. She figured he was always hungry, and that was inscribed in his flesh as soon as he was born. Growing up in wartime Holland and then through the hungry winter of 1944–45 without enough food anywhere deepened that body hunger.

Henri knew also that he had always felt uneasy in his own body, that his body had yearnings and desires that he never dared to put into words. His body wanted more freedom. Even as a teenager, he wanted to be like trapeze artists, part of the freedom and transcendence of an artistic physical community.

.••••

HENRI IS SEIZED WITH a desire to tell Dennie more about himself. Surely Dennie would be interested to know about the Flying Rodleighs. An interviewer in 1995 asked Henri, "How will you apply the principles of the Flying Rodleighs in your life in the years to come?" And Henri had responded with enthusiasm, *"One principle is that I'd like to be freer. Just take more risks, you know, and trust that. And actually that has happened. In a very deep way just doing this crazy thing, for me to rent a camper and to go travelling through Germany with the circus—that's a little crazy in the first place, certainly when you're over sixty years old. On a deeper level, I mean, it has given me a sense that my life is just beginning."*

But even though Dennie's attention is focused on Henri's body, Henri is feeling too tired to explain all this. And anyway, traveling with the Flying Rodleighs came later.

4

C. S. Lewis wrote in *A Grief Observed* that no one had ever told him that grief felt so much like fear, "the same fluttering in the stomach, the same restlessness . . . I keep on swallowing." Henri swallows. His feelings in the hotel room seem like fear, but they are also like something else, oddly like the excitement that gripped him five years earlier. No one ever told Henri that fear feels so much like adolescent desire, the same pounding of his heart, the queasy feeling in his gut, the uneasy restless twitching, the unsettling emotion overflowing into tears. His body's responses now in Hilversum are not so different from what he had felt in 1991 when he first encountered the Flying Rodleighs.

·····

Looking at the pictures of the five artists in the circus program, I found myself wondering about the ways these lives had become connected and given shape to their ten minutes of air ballet. I said to myself: "Who is Rodleigh? Who is Jennie? Who is Karlene?

Who is Johan? Who is Jon? Who are these people flying and catching in a circus tent somewhere in Germany? I wish I could talk to them, look closely at them, touch them and maybe become their friend."

I was embarrassed by my own desires, but simply decided not to let my embarrassment bother me too much. After all, . . . nobody was looking, . . . far from home, . . . far from work, . . . far from duties and obligations, . . . far from the regular pattern of my life. Why not be a teenager, a fan, an all-out admirer? What did I have to lose?

It is clear from all these inner ruminations that I was having a difficult time dealing with my stirred-up emotions. A little later, as I walked with my Franciscan hosts to the circus, I kept thinking: "I wonder how I could get to meet these artists? Will they be open to see me, to talk to me, to give their time and attention, or will they just treat me as one of their many fans who ask curious but foolish questions and who have to be whisked away like bees from a jar of marmalade?" I realized that my Franciscan companions had none of these questions and certainly wouldn't understand them.

As we walked through the entranceway, decorated with hundreds of little lights, bright pictures of lions and tigers and the faces of clowns, I noticed the circus director, Gerd Simoneit, standing there. The moment I saw him I knew that this was my chance to find a way to the circus group. As my companions walked on into the circus tent to find their seats, I walked up to him and said in German: "Good evening, sir. I saw your show a few nights ago and really enjoyed it, especially the Flying Rodleighs. I wonder if there is any chance of meeting the artists?"

His response was very surprising. Pointing to a woman with a small girl passing in front of the popcorn and soft drinks stand, he said: "That's one of them; why don't you ask her?"

Karlene was uneasy when the circus owner, Mr. Simoneit, pointed at her. Circus rules meant that she should not be out front where patrons could see her wearing her makeup, but she had promised her daughter Kail an ice cream from the refreshment wagon. Instead of a reprimand, Simoneit sent a tall, slender, middle-aged Dutchman bounding over to her.

"Hello, do you speak English?" he asked.

"Oh yes," she said, "I am from South Africa."

He was beaming with such joy and she was so relieved, that he immediately felt like an old friend. Her small daughter Kail, busy with her ice cream, ignored them. Amused by Henri's nearly inarticulate admiration and his clear desire to meet the troupe, Karlene invited him backstage to meet all of them during the intermission after their performance. She figured such a starstruck, gray-haired fan would entertain her brother Rodleigh. Then she and Kail hurried out of sight to the privacy of the backstage area.

As I walked back to the circus tent trying to find where my Franciscan friends had gone, I felt as if I had just taken a huge jump. It seemed as if I had just done something I had thought myself incapable of doing,—as if I had broken some kind of dangerous taboo. After having found my companions, I focused my attention on the director, Gerd Simoneit, who walked, microphone in hand, into the middle of the ring and announced the first act: Sascha Houke and his Arabian stallions. But my mind was elsewhere. Impatiently, I sat through the stallion act and the different acts that followed. Finally, more than forty minutes later, a group of Moroccans carried in the large net and with amazing speed built it up above the whole ring with large aprons on both ends, reaching to the far ends of the tent.

A clown tried to keep us occupied while everything was made ready for the trapeze act. Then, with great aplomb, the director announced the "dangerous, spectacular and aesthetically pleasing performance of . . . (here he paused to heighten the tension) . . . the Flying Rodleighs." To great applause they entered the ring, swirled their silver capes, took them off, lifted themselves into the net, climbed the rope ladder, and started their performance.

Once again I was completely captivated by the dazzling acrobatics, but this time I felt a strange fear. Having spoken with Karlene and knowing that I would meet them all within a few minutes, I had the strange sensation of worrying about their well-being. "I hope all goes well. I hope they won't make any mistakes," I kept thinking. Then it happened. As Karlene flew down from the top of the tent to be caught by her catcher, I saw that something had gone wrong. My body tensed up as I saw Karlene missing the catcher's hands and plunging down into the net. The net threw her body back up until it fell again and came to rest. The audience gasped but quickly relaxed when it saw Karlene straighten up, jump from the net, walk to the rope ladder, and climb back up to continue the show.

Henri's whole body shivers, remembering the distress he felt imagining the emotions of such a dangerous physical performance, an act permeated with the ever-present possibility of failure. Karlene simply climbed back up the ladder and carried on, but Henri found his own emotional response almost unbearable. It wasn't just the physical fall, but rather the possibility of public humiliation, of being judged harshly by a disappointed audience.

After that I could hardly watch anymore. I knew that the woman I had met for a few seconds at the concession stand was all right, but I was suddenly confronted with the other side of this air-ballet, not simply the dangers of physical harm, but the experience of failure, shame, guilt, frustration, and anger.

5

Dennie, seeing Henri shiver, interrupts his reverie. "Okay, the fire department will bring a stretcher up to us. The window for moving is down the hall, and we can take you there when they arrive. That window is big enough for your stretcher, so we will slide you out the window onto a lift mounted on a fire truck. I will stay with you as the lift lowers you to the ground."

For a moment, Henri wonders if he is having a bizarre dream, the kind of strange dreams that come when he forgets to take his nightly anti-anxiety medication. He has used Ativan for more than seven years, though he has considered trying to wean himself off it.

Just six months earlier, while waiting for spring to arrive, he raised the question of his medication with the doctor in New Jersey whom he had been seeing during his sabbatical. He explained that he was troubled by his experience after a fine lunch and animated discussion with friends.

"When I came home I felt quite weary. Tired, dizzy and out of focus. I realized that this was caused by not taking the Ativan tablet before going to bed each night," Henri told his doctor. *"Since I wasn't sure whether or not I had*

taken the tablet, I did not dare take another." His voice trailed off, until he gathered his thoughts again. *"I think I have become addicted to it since my surgery in January 1989. Without the tablet, I get wild dreams and sleep rest-lessly and anxiously. So the whole day I felt out of sorts and without motivation."*

His doctor nodded in understanding, then responded. "If you want to go off Ativan, you will need to be willing to feel like that for at least two weeks."

Henri pondered this. *"I am not yet willing to do it,"* he finally admit-ted. *"It seems such a waste of time and energy."*

Later that day, he carefully wrote about that conversation with his doctor in the publishable journal he kept during his sabbatical. Maybe readers might find this confession of vulnerability helpful, he thought. Many people depend on all kinds of medication to be well in their lives, and perhaps they will feel less alone knowing that he shares this experience. Writing about shared human experiences is part of his ministry, a way of laying down his life for others.

Now he vaguely wonders if other people have dreams of athletic paramedics throwing them out windows when they forget to take their medication. But no, he realizes, this is not a dream. He really is at a hotel in Hilversum, waiting for the fire department to arrive.

Suddenly Henri feels afraid, queasy with anxiety. It is one thing to say, as he often had, that the movement of his life has been from his mind as a popular professor, to his heart living in community with people with intellectual disabilities, to more recently discov-ering his body in a new way. The elegant movement from head to heart to body sounded convincing when he was standing firmly on the ground. But now his mind is spinning, his heart is apparently failing, and his body is about to be pushed out a window. Defenes-trated. Alone.

He forces himself to think instead about that breathless first day of meeting his new friends.

.••••

As soon as the artists had concluded their performance, received the applause, and disappeared behind the curtains, I excused myself to my companions and found my way to the back of the tent.

In a dark corner of the backstage area, the five artists were putting on their sweatsuits. When Karlene saw me she signaled me to come closer and told the group that we had met before the show and that she had invited me to join them after the act. There were no formal introductions. They just said "hello" and let me be there while they discussed their performance.

Rodleigh sighed as he headed backstage, ready to review why Karlene had missed her catch. When there was a failure, it was especially important to figure out what had happened so they would not repeat the mistake.

Joining the rest of the troupe, Rodleigh was not entirely pleased to see that a stranger had joined them, especially on a day when the act was flawed. Now they would not be able to discuss it in private. Oh well, he thought, I will explain that he can stay if he listens quietly and respectfully. We have work to do.

Rodleigh's sister Karlene introduced them to her new friend Henri, and Rodleigh found his ill humor soothed by Henri's heartfelt admiration and compliments. Then the troupe stood in a circle to discuss the performance, and Henri leapt right into the middle of their circle and interrupted with a barrage of questions, his large hands flailing. Annoyed yet also amused, Rodleigh kept trying to quiet Henri's excitement, but he persisted in standing right in front of each person so that they could not see each other. Yet it was hard to hold irritation. The offense was so unintentional, and Henri's facial expressions so comical that before the end of the meeting all five trapeze artists were laughing. Henri did not seem to mind. In fact, their mirth made him feel at home. When Rodleigh asked Henri why he stood right in front of the person talking, Henri explained that he could not hear their unfamiliar words very well and wanted to focus on the person talking. Rodleigh accepted the explanation and decided that if he ever met Henri again, he would remember to talk loudly and more clearly.

Listening to their exchange of words, I realized that I had entered a completely new world. Although they spoke clear English, I could not fully understand a single sentence. I picked up words such as "hop up," "lay out," "passage," "cradle" and other expressions which I couldn't even pronounce, let alone comprehend. It was clear, however, that every part of the ten-minute act was analyzed and evaluated in detail. No great issue was made of Karlene's fall into the net, even though that was what preoccupied me the most. They talked about it, but only as one aspect of a long, complicated routine.

After this discussion the group left the tent and moved in the direction of their caravans. As I walked with them, one of the men turned to me and said, "I am Rodleigh . . . well, this is your chance to ask me your questions." As he said this, I felt a certain distance and even fear of being an unwelcome intruder, and I really didn't have any particular questions. So I said, "Well, I was so moved by your

*act that I wanted to meet you and maybe understand a little bet-
ter what your art is all about. . . . I really do not have any special
questions. I know too little to have any questions."*

Seeing that Henri seemed determined to find out everything about
the circus and the Flying Rodleighs' act in just one meeting, Rodleigh
tried the old trick of turning the tables and instead asked Henri what
he did for a living.

"I am a priest and I work in Canada with handicapped people
and I write books," responded Henri.

Rodleigh stared with astonishment. It wasn't an answer he had
expected from the tall, balding man with his helpless look of chronic
confusion. He warmed to Henri's sparkling eyes, enormous behind his
thick glasses, and his wide, eager smile.

He realized, however, that the fastest way to send Henri back to
his seat would be to invite him to their practice the next day.

*Rodleigh smiled and said: "If you'd like to, come to our practice
here tomorrow morning at eleven, and you can see for yourself what
it's all about!" I looked at him not fully believing the invitation. Why
did he invite me? Why did he want me to come and see for myself? It
seemed that Rodleigh took my interest in their profession more seriously than I had taken it myself. But with all my inner questioning
there was little doubt about the answer: "I'd love to come," I said
quickly. "Thank you for asking me. For sure I will be there tomorrow
at eleven."*

Rodleigh hurried back to his caravan, entertained by the curious
interlude. He didn't really expect Henri would show up the next day.

As the five went through the little gate that separated the tent area from the caravan park, I waved them good-bye. "See you tomorrow," and found my way back into the tent where my Franciscan friends stood wondering where I had gone during the intermission. I didn't tell them. I just sat there silently looking at the tigers, the lions, the clown, and the tumblers. My mind wasn't there. I just kept wondering what my little visit during the intermission had set in motion.

As the circus band played their tunes and one act followed the other, I realized that I had already made my decision: as long as the Flying Rodleighs were in town, I was going to see them every chance I had, whether they were practicing or performing. I knew I had found something that was going to take me a big step closer to the understanding of the mystery of being alive! Everyone else may call the circus a nice distraction or a welcome interruption, but I decided to call it a new vocation!

As I awoke from my daydreams, I noticed that the director Gerd Simoneit was calling all the artists into the ring for the "finale." There I saw them again; looking bright and shiny in their red and gold decorated costumes, they waved to the cheering public. And as the Flying Rodleighs stood there waving among the lion tamers, clowns, equilibrists, stallion trainers, and tumblers, I felt tears welling up in my eyes. I knew that this evening would be the beginning of a new spiritual adventure, the end of which was known only to God.

It was an unexpectedly emotional experience, and while an emotional response was central to the story he was writing, Henri was still groping to understand and articulate it. He knew that some readers thought that he revealed too much, that he poured out his inner life indiscriminately, but he also knew that was a mirage, a persona that was truthful but not complete. Henri was careful about what he put into writing. He decided to finish the story of that evening.

While returning to the Franciscan convent, the superior and his student had little to say about the evening. They said they had enjoyed it, but their conversation quickly shifted to other subjects. I didn't tell them about my "secret." How could I explain to them that I was planning to go to the circus at least twice a day! Well, I didn't have to! I enjoyed having a little secret just as much as when I was a little boy digging tunnels in the backyard of my parents' home and hiding my treasures there.

That night I didn't sleep too well. In my mind I kept looking upwards and seeing two women and three men moving freely through the air and I thought: "Isn't that what life is all about—flying and catching!" I knew my father would agree.

Would his readers understand the dramatic irony of his narrative, that he was describing his "little secret," sharing the treasure that he was claiming to have hidden? That he was in some ways still that little boy, with secrets but also wanting his father to approve? Henri liked secrets, and thinking was safe. He had not tried to write down everything.

II

Falling

6

Fear and excitement can feel the same, thinks Henri on his bed at Hotel Lapershock, restlessly breathing through the pain around his heart. He wants his father. His father's weak heart has worried him, but perhaps his own is in worse shape. How strange. Even though his father is now ninety-three, Henri knows he would come quickly, and wonders if he himself will forever be a prodigal son who lives far from his father but longs for him.

WHEN HENRI HAD A serious accident in 1988, his father flew across the ocean to be with him. Henri almost died of internal bleeding after being hit by the side mirror of a van while foolishly rushing on foot along the slippery edge of a busy, icy road north of Toronto. *Everything has changed,* he thought at that time. *None of my plans matter anymore. It is awful, painful, but maybe very good.*

That accident happened because he was trying to do too much, to prove that he could outmaneuver the winter weather and keep his planned commitments regardless of physical limitations. But on that cold morning as he lay in semidarkness by the side of the road, he felt *as if some strong hand had stopped me and forced me into a kind of necessary surrender.* In the following hours, full of intravenous tubes and surrounded by monitors, he was surprised that his feeling of powerlessness did not frighten him. Faced with the possibility of dying, he felt quite safe in his hospital bed with its railings on both sides. *Notwithstanding the severe pain, I had a completely unexpected sense of security.*

As he recovered from that accident, he observed how the most profound shifts in his life were due to interruptions. *A long time of solitude in a Trappist monastery interrupting a busy life of teaching, a confrontation with poverty in Latin America interrupting a rather comfortable life in the North, a call to live with mentally handicapped people interrupting an academic career.* Those were intentional interruptions. After all, as he liked to say, he is Dutch, with an impatient disposition and a need to be in control. He meticulously planned those key "interruptions." Other interruptions he chose spontaneously, such as Martin Luther King Jr.'s 1965 march in Selma that interrupted his studies in psychology at the Menninger Clinic in Kansas.

More disorienting had been unexpected interruptions, like the sudden death of his mother, or the breakage of a deep friendship that so completely shattered his sense of emotional safety that Henri spent months recovering in therapeutic retreat settings.

Oddly, the physical accident in 1988 that almost killed him had been less traumatic. The greater trauma was recovering. Before the surgery, he had worked to make peace with his life and impending death. After believing that he had wrapped up his life in reconciliation and goodwill, his recovery felt anticlimactic, even depressing as he resumed the various complicated relationships of his life.

NOW IN 1996, WAITING with Dennie in his hotel room, Henri doesn't feel near death. He feels somewhat relieved by this interruption of his journey. He is pausing in Holland on his way to Russia, where he is scheduled to be filmed discussing Rembrandt's painting *The Return of the Prodigal Son*. The actual painting is enormous, more than half again as tall as Henri and many times wider. It will make a dramatic backdrop as Henri tells the story of the first time he saw the painting more than a decade ago, remaining in front of it for so long that eventually an official at the Hermitage Museum in St. Petersburg gave him his own special chair.

For this film, he plans to explain the dynamics of the painting, vividly reiterating many of the same points he made in his book *The Return of the Prodigal Son*. Henri looks forward to seeing the actual painting again, but has dreaded the trip. He is tired. He has not rested since arriving back in his community two weeks earlier after a busy sabbatical year. That sabbatical year was designed as a time to rest and write, but instead became a year full of stimulating travel, new friendships, and emotional complications. He has not felt ready to travel again so soon. Perhaps this interruption will turn out well.

Right now his chest aches severely and he can't deny that the sensation in his gut feels like fear. He tries to reinterpret the queasy feeling as excitement or desire. But combined with the unnerving pain in his chest, he can't remember what he might desire in these circumstances. Just to reach the ground safely. He offers that thought up as a small prayer. Prayer is to be fully present where you are, even for a moment, he has often announced. So now he wills himself to put everything else out of his mind and be fully present, like a trapeze artist in flight.

He lets go of the trip to Russia that is now interrupted. He puts out of his mind . . .

But actually, he realizes, he has no desire to be fully present in this insecure moment. He really wants to be fully present in a different time entirely, remembering what happened next after he met the Flying Rodleighs. He lets his mind shift back again to 1991, back to the day he first went to see the Rodleighs practice.

•••••

"I am here to write, not to go to the circus!" I kept saying to myself. "I came all the way from Canada to have the quiet time to read, reflect and write about the life of the Spirit. I want to be alone, free from distractions and interruptions, and here I am accepting an invitation to watch the practice of a group of trapeze artists!"

The next morning while sitting at my desk, I kept looking at my watch. I couldn't concentrate on my writing. I could think of nothing but meeting the Flying Rodleighs again at their practice session at eleven o'clock. "What would it be like meeting them again? Would they be kind to me?" I was acutely aware that I had made them into some kind of unapproachable stars. The admiring child in me was so impressed by their invitation to come to their practice that everything else seemed less important.

At ten thirty I took the streetcar and a little before eleven I walked into the big tent. What a difference from last night! No audience— only empty seats.

RODLEIGH WAS EAGER TO work on his new routine that morning. He knew this first practice would include a lot of falls, because he would fly and be caught three times before returning to the pedestal board. Each attempt would be recorded on video so that he and the other troupe members could analyze what went wrong, then problem-solve how to improve. The timing was complicated and required precision, but the innovative sequence was exciting, and Rodleigh liked challenges. He would not have been surprised if Henri had not shown up at their practice session, but at eleven Henri was already pacing about, impatiently waiting for something to happen.

I waited for the Flying Rodleighs to appear. At eleven Rodleigh walked into the tent. He saw me and came up to me. "Good morning," he said. Pointing to one of the benches around the ring he said: "Why don't you sit down there. Karlene will be with you in a minute, and she will explain to you what you want to know."

His friendly, matter-of-fact attitude put me at ease. He was dressed in black tights and a T-shirt. Soon after Sascha and his horses had left the ring, the two other men of the trapeze troupe appeared and started to help Rodleigh set up the net. Then I noticed Karlene and her daughter and the other woman; they all looked more like maintenance people than artists.

Karlene came to me. "How are you this morning?" she asked. "Great," I said, "happy to be here." Karlene was carrying a little video recorder. "Looks like you are going to make a film," I said, somewhat surprised by this technological side to the practice session.

Meanwhile, the net was in position, and everyone, except Kar-

lene, was in place, high up in the tent. "Can you tell me, who is who?" I asked. "Sure, I am glad to," she said. "Well, you know my brother Rodleigh; he started the group. That's him, standing there on the pedestal board. With him, standing there, is his wife Jennie. And there high up on the center catch bar is Jon. He is from Detroit. He joined us a few years ago. And at the right, up there sitting in his catch trap is Joe. He is from South Africa like Rodleigh, Jennie, and me."

The little girl Kail climbed out from underneath the bleachers and assessed the tall stranger who was talking with her mother. She had met many new adult friends in her four years. This one looked promising. His hands were busy moving and his eyes were big and kind. She had just finished creating a sawdust cake. Standing directly in front of him so that he could not ignore her, she announced loudly, "I am making a birthday cake, and you have to pretend that it tastes good. Come and look!" Henri looked surprised, but he obediently followed her to the sawdust pile, where she had arranged two sticks as candles in her cake. "Now you have to pretend you have a fork and eat it." "Okay," Henri said. After following her instructions, he announced, *"It really tastes very good. You know how to make a good cake."* Kail beamed. But he seemed a bit too sincere. Maybe he would get confused and actually eat the cake, so she clarified, "We are only pretending, you know."

When I looked up from my little game with Kail, I saw Jennie falling into the net. She was wearing a safety belt with long ropes that came through pulleys high up in the tent. Rodleigh was standing on the floor now, holding the ropes. She had missed a trick and Rodleigh had broken her fall by pulling the ropes. He walked up to Karlene and replayed the video to see what had gone wrong; then he asked Jennie to try again.

Karlene said to me: "We are trying some new tricks. It always takes a long time to learn something new. But Rodleigh wants to keep improving our act. Some artists never change their act once they master it, but Rodleigh keeps trying new things."

"How long have you been doing this?" I asked.

"Oh. I am completely new at it. I just joined Rodleigh a little over a year ago. I was living in Hawaii with Kail. One day he called me and said: 'Why don't you come over, and I will teach you the trapeze.' I had been teaching athletics to little kids for some years and was ready for a change. Well, I flew over to Germany and Rodleigh immediately started training me at winter quarters in Einbeck. As teenagers we had done a lot of things together, but nothing like this. At first I was very scared, but I learned quickly. After a few months, Rodleigh put me in the flying act, and when our other flyer left, I had to take over from him. Anyhow, it's all quite new for me."

"My goodness, you learned all these things you were doing last night, in such a short time," I said, not hiding my amazement.

"Yes," she replied. "I was already past my thirties when I started to do flying trapeze, but Rodleigh said I could do it, and he kept encouraging me. Well, I like it, although after a fall like last night, I feel like I'm ready to quit."

While Rodleigh, Jon, Joe, and Jennie practiced and Karlene recorded the different tricks, I got my first impressions of these artists' life outside the limelight. During a free moment, Rodleigh said, with a smile: "Ten minutes in the air requires a lot of work. I hope you are becoming aware of it." I believed him but was still too new to know exactly what he meant. I understood that a good trapeze act requires much practice, but Rodleigh suggested that there was a lot more going on outside showtime than I knew.

Suddenly, I started to sense a burning desire to know, not just a little bit, but everything. One question after another piled up in my mind: "Who really are these people? What got them interested in doing these tricks? What brought them together? How are they living together going from town to town in Germany?"

7

Henri's breathing quickens as he relives the excitement of getting to know the Flying Rodleighs—his eager restlessness, the sense of being on the verge of a new discovery, his amazed thrill over meeting these remarkable artists—his adolescent infatuation—oh yes, those days were all so stimulating!

Dennie studies Henri. His breathing is becoming more rapid. He is probably frightened as well as in pain. Dennie puts his hand gently on Henri's arm to calm him. "Don't worry. We are looking after you. Breathe with me and it will help you to feel better."

Henri tries to focus, to breathe slowly in rhythm with Dennie. In, two, three, and out, two, three. Slowly. In, two, three, and out, two, three.

After a few breaths, he feels more connected with Dennie. He appreciates Dennie's gentle kindness and wonders how and when he decided to become a nurse. It seems like too much effort to ask.

"That's better," Dennie encourages him. "Now I am going to start you on oxygen. I need to take your glasses off to put the mask on."

Henri closes his eyes and remembers the first days of getting to know the Flying Rodleighs, a time when opening a window seemed like an agreeable and uncomplicated metaphor.

·····•

Is this trapeze act perhaps one of the windows in the house of life that opens up a view to a totally new enrapturing landscape? Henri wondered as he watched the practice that morning.

And then there were all those other questions about the choices these men and women had made.

"Wasn't Rodleigh a medical technician, Jennie a nurse, and Kar-lene a teacher? What made them decide to leave their jobs and their countries and become flyers in a circus? And what about Joe and Jon, the catchers?" I really knew nothing about them and felt an urge to know the hows and the whats, the wheres and the whys of their lives.

Was this mere curiosity? Was I just prying into the lives of a group of strangers? I didn't know how to answer these questions, but I re-alized that the more I saw, the more I wanted to see and the more I knew, the more I wanted to know. I trusted that there was much more going on in me than curiosity. Wasn't the ten-minute spectacle of these five people in midair like a living painting put together by great artists?

I had spent days, years, studying the lives of Rembrandt van Rijn and Vincent van Gogh. I was not content just seeing their draw-ings and paintings. I wanted to know who these men were that had created works gazed upon by thousands of people day after day. And aren't these ten minutes of air-ballet like a painting made by five painters, a painting that keeps thousands of people, young and old, spellbound every afternoon and evening?

Nobody seemed to find it strange when I showed interest in the personal lives of Rembrandt and Vincent. And I had to get it all from books. They can't be spoken with. And here are five people drawing in the air—colorful, gracious, and most harmonious lines—while lifting up the hearts of so many! Is it no more than curiosity to want to know what is behind this perfect picture? Might it not be the desire to know the secret of the beauty and truth of human life?

THE PRACTICE ENDED. RODLEIGH and the other men rolled up the net, then bid farewell to Henri and watched him leave the circus grounds. Henri charged off, obviously late for his lunch. Rodleigh guessed that Henri's mind was full of new thoughts, and he chuckled as Henri almost tripped over a cable but didn't seem to notice. Rodleigh shook his head, still smiling as he walked back to his caravan, relieved that he would not have to answer Henri's questions that day.

When I took the streetcar back to the Franciscan convent, I was no longer wondering about my motives. I was convinced that the encounter with these five artists had indeed opened a new window in my life and that it would be very sad if I didn't look through it as long and attentively as I could.

Right there, in the streetcar going home, I decided to go to all the practice sessions, all the shows, and all the evaluation meetings. As long as the Flying Rodleighs were in town, I was going to be there, trusting that the landscape I would see would be worth all the time and effort.

At lunch I didn't mention my decision. After all, the Flying Rodleighs weren't as acceptable as Rembrandt or van Gogh, and I had no desire to prove to anybody that they were worth so much of my time and energy. After lunch, I went to bed and fell into a deep sleep. I knew I had found a treasure in a field. Now I needed to hide the treasure, see what I had, and then buy the field! When I woke from my nap, I felt glad to know that tonight I was going to the circus again!

After the evening show, the catcher Jon Griggs said to me: "I guess you like our show!" "I sure do," I said. "Every time I see it again, I like it more." Jon seemed at ease with my interest and quite eager to talk. "People seldom come to us after the show," he observed. "Maybe they are too shy. During intermission, they want to see the animals,— not us! And by the time the whole program is over, they have seen so many acts that they have already forgotten about the trapeze. I guess that's normal. That's circus life."

As we walked to the trailers Jon said: "You want to see my place?" "Sure," I said. I entered the trailer and noticed how small it was. There was a large colored photograph showing Rodleigh, Jennie, Karlene, Joe, and Jon in their trapeze costumes. "Nice picture," I said. "Yes, that's us," he answered proudly.

I was impressed with how easy it was to talk with Jon. No distance, no pretensions, no hesitations. He was so easy and self-confident. "Can I invite you for lunch someday?" I asked. "Then we can talk more."

"Yes, that would be great. Let me see. What about Saturday at noon? We have no practice and I don't have to be here before the afternoon show."

"Saturday is fine for me," I said. "I will pick you up here at

11:30, okay?" Jon seemed happy with the invitation, and I was ex-cited with the chance to ask him many questions about catching and how he learned it.

Over the next days, Jennie and Rodleigh invited Henri for lunch and as a gift Henri brought them some of the books he had written. They thanked him warmly, and placed them on a shelf. After the matinee act, Rodleigh found Henri beaming with joy backstage, as eager to celebrate the successful act as if he had been part of it. Flip-ping through the books later, Rodleigh was perplexed to discover that the funny, gangly man who always looked like he would walk home in the wrong direction had been a professor of theology and psychology at some of the most prestigious universities in the United States.

Rodleigh now began to ask the same question that Henri himself was trying to resolve: Why was Henri so interested in the trapeze?

8

Henri had always been mesmerized by artists. Beauty, discipline, skill—all kinds of artistic endeavor enthralled him. Even the dramatic way that Rodleigh ended each performance was thrilling:

> At the very end, they let themselves fall into the net all the way from the top. Rod, the last one, when he dives into the net—the net is like a trampoline—it throws him back up so high that he can catch the swing again. People aren't expecting that. So he comes down in the net and he falls all the way down, but then the net throws him back up so high that he catches the swing. So you think he's down, and he's up again.

Physical artistry and that kind of connection with an audience especially gripped Henri. He recalled one night in Holland in the mid-1980s. Staying at his father's home, he had been captivated by the artistic energy of two quite different performances when he came upon them playing at the same time on different television channels.

On one channel a rock concert with Tina Turner and David Bowie in Birmingham, England, was shown. On the other St. Matthew's Passion was performed in the St. Peter's Church in Leiden. I kept changing channels since I felt a strange attraction to both.

Tina Turner and David Bowie sang a song in front of a huge crowd of young people waving arms: "It is only love," or something like that. They sang with their whole bodies in such an increasingly gutsy way that they brought their audience gradually into a state of collective ecstasy: a sea of moving bodies, hands raised, eyes closed, totally surrendering to the sensual rhythm of the drumbeat. On the stage Tina and David held each other in a complex embrace while screaming their passionate song into their handheld microphones. Tina Turner's dress and movements were unambiguously meant to evoke sexual feelings; her dramatic staring into David Bowie's child-like clean-shaven face drove the crowd to a climactic frenzy. As they built up the tension with their lips nearly kissing, while screaming, "It is only love," the crowd merged into one dazed, anonymous being in the grip of these powerful feelings.

As I switched the channel I heard the voice of the Evangelist singing the passion of Jesus. Jesus stood before Pilate, silently, and the people cried: "Let Barabbas go, crucify Jesus." The choir sang the beautiful Bach chorales which meditate upon the divine love of our Savior. I thought, "It is only love," and felt a deep sadness invading me. The members of the choir were all above 40 years of age, dressed in formal black dresses, suits, white shirts, and ties. They looked stiff and serious while singing the sacred words of Jesus, their bodies remaining completely motionless. Only the director let his body move with the waves of Bach's melodies. The TV cameras never showed an *audience. Once in a while they pointed to the splendid architecture of the church and dwelled for a moment upon the ornate candelabra's soft yellow light.*

I switched back to Tina and David. She was back on the stage for another song with David. She was dressed differently. She said to her applauding fans, "Hi folks, sorry for letting you wait. I had to make myself pretty for you again . . . are you all ready for the next one?" And thousands of voices screamed, "Yea . . ." As the half-nude muscular drummer started to beat his huge drums the crowd turned back into that strange no-man's-land of dreams and desire, arms raised up, eyes closed, feet stomping.

Now the Bach choir sang, "Rest softly, Lord. Rest quietly. Your passion has come to an end. Have a great rest, dear Savior." Slowly the cameras moved back and gave a last view in the church as the final notes were sung. Then all was still for a moment and the program closed.

Meanwhile thousands clapped, yelled, stamped, and screamed as Tina and David held hands and bowed, jumped, laughed, and threw kisses into the Birmingham music hall. Both performances ended at the same time.

Henri sat clutching his elbows, nearly speechless. As a priest and a European, he felt an affinity with the profoundly beautiful and spiritual Bach concert. But the overt sexual energy of the other performance really grabbed him.

I sat there in my father's living room unable to grasp what I had seen. I felt part of both and distant from both events. Henri concluded, *I was exhausted and wondered what it all meant to see this at home with my father.*

He found himself wishing he could be in the huge, anonymous

Birmingham audience. Or even be on that stage. The physical energy he brought to his university lectures made him a popular professor, he knew, but there was a joyful freedom in Tina Turner and David Bowie's performance that he could hardly fathom. What would it be like to perform with that kind of utter conviction and uninhibited physical engagement?

Five years later in Freiburg, Henri and his father again joined an audience, and Henri was again overwhelmed by the physical power of a performance. This time Henri fell in love with an entire trapeze troupe. Not only did he want to get to know them and understand every detail of their act, but the rush of creative energy awoke his own yearning to be an artist himself—as a writer.

9

For the next few days, I kept going to the circus as often as possible. I attended the practice session, saw the afternoon or evening shows, sometimes both.

Henri urgently wanted to understand everything about the trapeze act, but found the details confusing. Rodleigh sat beside Henri, sketching the rigging in Henri's notebook and patiently repeating himself, often explaining the same material as the day before.

I gradually began to feel a little bit like an insider, at least as far as the Rodleighs were concerned. One day Rodleigh said: "I hope you don't pay each time you come to a performance. Just tell the box office people that we invited you. They will let you in." I did what he said, and, indeed, they let me in without a ticket. Meanwhile, I had become a familiar face to the entrance attendants, so I hardly needed to explain.

Once after an evaluation get-together, I tried to strike up a conversation with Joe, the South African catcher. While Jon, the American, worked from the center catch bar, Joe's place was on the swinging catch bar, opposite the pedestal board. Joe's muscular appearance, rough facial features, and dark tan made him look more like an ironworker than a trapeze artist. He always seemed a little off by himself and maybe a little shy.

"How did you feel about the show this time?" I asked him.

"Oh, fine," he said. "Rodleigh was just a little early so I had to adjust my swing a bit to catch him but it was fine."

I realized that I didn't understand what being early or late meant, but it was clear that it was the real issue for the catcher. Joe's speech was very difficult. He stutters heavily and isn't very talkative. But once I approached him, he was quite eager to speak.

"Do you like your job?" I asked.

He smiled at me and said very emphatically: "I love it. I love being in the catch bar and catching them!"

It was clear he meant what he said. Having seen the act many times, I became aware of the unique role of the catcher.

"You are not as much in the limelight as the flyers, but without you nothing can happen," I said.

He was quick to respond. "I really like it that way. The flyer gets all the attention, but their lives depend on the catcher! I don't want all the applause. I like what I am doing, and I have to give it all I've got. It's an important job to catch, and I love it, but I am glad to be a little less visible than the rest of them."

Henri wanted to stay backstage to watch the troupe warm up for the afternoon show, but he could not restrain himself from coming too close to their swinging arms to ask questions and try to carry on conversations. Finally Rodleigh sent him back inside the tent for his own safety.

That day, Rodleigh's new act did not go well and he fell into the front net, called the apron. Henri was alarmed seeing the fall, relieved to see that Rodleigh was not injured, and dismayed later to see all Rodleigh's painful red scratches from the nylon net.

"Why do you risk serious injury?" Henri asked. He was not entirely placated when Rodleigh responded with a string of stories about many previous accidents, although Rodleigh assured him that they overcame these mishaps through perseverance and hard work. Henri left perplexed, thinking all the way home about the hard and unusual life of circus performers.

The next day, Henri's questions took on a new tone.

"Why are you choosing to do a high-risk routine rather than something more predictable and safe?" he asked.

Rodleigh felt a bit defensive, but he knew that what sounded like criticism of the performance was concern for their safety. "The circus business is very competitive, Henri," explained Rodleigh, "and if the circus director is not satisfied with the audience response, we will be replaced next season. My job is to find the balance between difficulty and control, and build the routine intelligently."

Henri was listening attentively, so Rodleigh continued. "Also we are artists. We are proud people. So as a personal challenge, I try to make the most difficult tricks and routine look easy—fluid and graceful. I want to make the audience focus not on the danger but on the beauty."

On Saturday morning I met Jon at his trailer. We took the street-car to downtown Freiburg. I had wondered where to take him for dinner. The only place which seemed quiet enough for a good conversation was the "Red Bears," where my father had stayed. So I had made a reservation for 12:30. Since we were a half hour early, I asked Jon if he had already seen the Munster, the splendid cathedral. He hadn't and I wondered if he had seen anything at all of this city since the circus arrived.

Of all the medieval churches, the Munster is probably the one that had most impressed me. Its fascinating history, its location in the center of the city square, its magnificent tower with filigreed stone spire, its intimate interior . . . I had fallen in love with the Munster as I had fallen in love with the city.

But as I crossed the square and walked into the cathedral with Jon, I suddenly felt completely paralyzed in trying to convey to him any of the emotions that filled my heart.

"What do you think?" I said.

"I like it," he answered, but it was clear he felt like a cat in cold water. I immediately realized that everything the church meant to me was strange to Jon. He walked through it with an odd sense of obligation. I had taken him there, so here he was, but nothing spoke to him. The pillars with the Twelve Apostles, the splendid triptych on the high altar, the richly carved choir stools, the sculpture of Our Lady with the sea of lit candles and people praying in front to of it . . . nothing spoke a word to him. I wanted to explain. But how do you explain medieval Christianity to a trapeze catcher from Detroit?

Soon we were in the Red Bears, still early, but more at ease. We ordered lunch. It was probably the most expensive lunch I had *ordered since coming to Freiburg. As I looked around and saw the middle-aged and older people in their formal dress and as the waiter filled our glasses, lit the table candle, and offered us napkins to put on our laps, I wondered if this was the most comfortable place for circus people to talk about flying and catching.*

However, as soon as we began to speak about the circus, the surroundings didn't seem to bother me anymore. They certainly didn't bother Jon.

"What is it that makes the circus so fascinating?" I asked.

"Well," said Jon, after a moment of silence, "I guess we like to see animals do what really only people can do and to see people do what really only animals can do. Lions sit up like people and people fly like birds."

The two of us laughed.

"The circus is a fun world. It offers clean entertainment, and it's for everybody, young and old."

"The circus certainly got me hooked," I said. "The last time I was in Freiburg I spent all my free time in churches and museums. This time it's the circus that caught my imagination."

"Yes," Jon observed, "you have become a real fan."

I felt a little awkward being called a fan, but I had to confess that the word suited me.

We spoke about many circus things, and Jon told me anything I wanted to know. He never asked about me. Maybe he simply doesn't know what to ask. Maybe I was just as strange to him as the Munster.

We were back at the circus around three o'clock. People were lining up in front of the box office for the afternoon performance, which was to begin in half an hour. I could see it was going to be a full house. At four twenty-five I stepped into the tent just in time to see the Flying Rodleighs walking into the ring and swirling their silver capes, accompanied by the orchestra. As I saw Jon climbing up the high rope ladder, bare chested, wearing white tights and a golden belt and then stepping on the catch bar high up in the dome of the tent, uttering a shout to excite his audience, I had a hard time believing that two hours earlier I sat with this demigod in the Red Bears eating lunch.

The act went flawlessly. When Rodleigh, Jennie, Karlene, Joe, and Jon paid their final compliments in the ring and disappeared behind the curtain to the accompaniment of the applause and foot stomping of the more than two thousand enthusiastic spectators, tears came to my eyes. I knew that I had become part of this group of strangers and that in some mysterious way, the huge applause also embraced me.

10

Henri's eyes are still closed. Dennie notes that his breathing is speeding up again. He looks like the kind of nervous person who could become agitated when the exit from the window begins.

"Henri?" he asks, "I could start some medication now. It will help you. There are two drugs in the drip. Droperidol will minimize your anxiety and tension, and fentanyl is a synthetic morphine to reduce your pain. The negative side effect is that it could lower your blood pressure even further, but I think you need it. What do you think?"

Henri seems far away. Dennie gently prods Henri for a response. Henri's eyes flicker open, large and bleary above the oxygen mask, and Dennie makes the decision to start the drip medication.

•••••

Sunday was the last day of the Circus Barum in Freiburg. After the afternoon show, as I was standing with the Rodleighs listening to their cryptic talk about the act, little Kail ran up to me and said: "Are you coming to see our trailer?" Karlene overheard her and said to me, "She really wants you to see our place. Come to us for a while after the finale."

An hour later, I was sitting with Karlene and Kail in their living room when Rodleigh knocked on the trailer door and invited me for supper along with Karlene and Kail. It was at supper that I first came to know Jennie. She welcomed me warmly around her small table.

"The trapeze is okay," she said, "but my real love is for making costumes."

As she spoke I became aware that all the costumes I had seen that week: the silver capes, the trapeze costumes, and the finale costumes were all made by Jennie.

"When I wanted to marry Rodleigh, I soon realized that becoming a trapeze artist was going to be part of the deal," she said smiling. "But I really got involved when I began to learn how to make our costumes. In the future, when we have become too old for the trapeze and we are going back to South Africa, I hope to start a business in costume design."

Jennie had nothing to hide. Spontaneous, direct, and very pragmatic, she made me feel right at home in the family. Here it all looked so normal and prosaic. Rodleigh, his wife, Jennie, his sister, Karlene, and the little Kail. That's the Stevens family in Germany. I was their guest for supper. Nothing special. Only that they all liked the flying trapeze.

After supper, Rodleigh said: "If you want to see something special, come tonight for 'pull-down.' Pull-down will show you how we disassemble our rigging while the Moroccans are taking down the tent. Forty-five minutes after the finale, we will be pulling out of the fairgrounds to the next town. Stay a little tonight until we leave. You will be impressed."

I did stay. During the intermission of the evening performance, Rodleigh, Joe, and Jon started already to load the truck with the net and the smaller parts of the trapeze rigging. Meanwhile, some of the animal wagons were already leaving the fairgrounds. But as soon as the finale was over, the whole place became a beehive of activity. Everyone knew exactly what to do. While the bleachers were taken down, the trapeze men started to disassemble the rigging. It was like a choreographed dance, meticulously planned and very quickly and carefully executed.

At five minutes to ten, Rodleigh closed his truck and connected it to the trailer. At the same time Jon and Joe were warming up their own trucks, and before I knew it, everyone was ready to leave.

"We are driving in convoy," Karlene explained. "Rodleigh leads, I follow, then Joe and then Jon. Rodleigh and Jon both have shortwave radios on their trucks, so that they can talk to each other on the road and keep an eye on what goes on between them. Once in a while, we lose each other because of stoplights and unexpected turns, but with the radios we can help each other to find our way back."

As Karlene spoke, I felt a sadness that I couldn't be part of that convoy. During the week, the Rodleighs had so much become part of my life that their leaving created a real pain in me. I realized too how difficult it must be for them to keep moving from place to place, never staying anywhere long enough to make lasting friends.

Was this the end? Would I see them again?

Then they began moving. I stood there waving at them all as they went into line and slowly turned out of the fairgrounds.

I felt lonely. Looking up, I saw the tent slowly coming down. It would take two hours to clear the place completely, but I had no desire to wait. Somehow, without the Rodleighs, the circus was just another circus, not worth staying up late for.

Walking away to catch a streetcar and go home, I felt a little confused. I still wasn't fully sure if I wasn't fooling myself with the new "vocation."

11

Dennie notices that despite the medication, Henri's body is still restlessly readjusting. He can't blame Henri for feeling unsettled. Being removed through a window is not a common occurrence.

But Henri is not thinking about his present state. He is back in 1991, remembering his sense of loneliness as he watched the Flying Rodleighs drive away and his sadness that he couldn't be part of that convoy. His legs twitch.

And now another memory is niggling for attention, drawing him back even further to another time when his whole body longed to join a community of people on the move together. As he wrote after the event, *It all began with a feeling of restlessness, an inner compulsion, a fierce gnawing, a painful question: Why aren't you in Selma?*

·····

IT WAS MARCH 1965, and Henri was studying psychology at the Menninger Clinic in Topeka, Kansas. Police in Alabama had used tear gas and violence to stop a peaceful civil rights march, and Martin Luther

King Jr. called for church leaders and people of faith from around the country to come to Selma, Alabama, for a new march. As a Dutch citizen on a visa, Henri had many reasons not to go. It was more than eight hundred miles away. His friends assured him that it was a local matter and he was a foreigner who should not get involved. They suggested that in going he would be serving just himself, looking for thrills and excitement. But Henri couldn't shake off his desire to respond.

The march started on Sunday, March 21. At eleven o'clock that night, Henri was tossing and turning in his bed when he suddenly realized that he had made a mistake. His choice became clear. By midnight he was in his Volkswagen Beetle heading toward the southern United States to join the marchers. *The restlessness disappeared, and there was a deep, palpable certainty and sense of determination.*

Seven hundred miles later in Vicksburg, Mississippi, Henri picked up a twenty-year-old hitchhiker named Charles. *As we drove through the night Charles told me about the dark days of Mississippi.* Charles was Black, and Henri assumed that Charles would now share his privilege as a White person, since Henri was the older of the two and the driver of the car. But he soon discovered that as a White man and a Black man traveling together, they could not safely stop anywhere. Not for gas, not for a coffee, not even to use a restroom. *Gradually I felt my innocence and unquestioned sense of freedom disappear,* Henri realized. The restlessness that had launched him onto this road trip returned full force, but this time embodied as fear. *The fear gave me new eyes, new ears, and a new mouth.* Eighteen hours after setting out, Henri and Charles arrived in Selma feeling grubby, unshaven, and tired. As they drove on to catch up with the march, the heavily armed National Guard lining the streets reminded Henri of growing up in occupied Holland during the war.

Arriving, they were greeted by two twelve-year-olds who were registering people for the march with three questions: What's your name? Where do you live? Who should we contact if anything happens to you? The third matter-of-fact question was unsettling, yet the overall feeling was not anxious. *No matter what the setting, people ate, laughed, talked, and prayed,* Henri wrote. Always hungry, he was especially impressed by the abundance of food. *It was one of the mysteries of Selma. Thousands were fed during those five days in Selma, in Montgomery, along the road, and in the tents; there was always enough. It seemed as if nothing had been organized and everything was always threatening to collapse in confusion, but somehow it always turned out all right. I realized what it's like to live with people who know the necessity of improvising and reacting with immediate spontaneity.*

Henri listened as on the steps of the Montgomery legislature, Martin Luther King Jr. spoke slowly and powerfully: "We are on the move." King's voice rose and gathered momentum as he named the struggle for human freedom in the history of his people, and the many martyrs whose deaths were not in vain because, he repeated, "We are on the move. We will go back and we will continue to suffer but now we know: we are on the move."

At exactly four o'clock, the jurisdiction of the troops to protect the marchers ended and fear again pervaded Henri's entire body. He offered a ride north to three Black men, who advised him all along the way to stick to the main roads, stay carefully within the speed limits, and not drive after dark. *I only remember that we were scared,* wrote Henri later, *scared to death, and that we shook all over whenever we rode through a city and were wary of every state trooper that we saw.*

The omnipresent danger, so familiar to his companions, shocked the thirty-three-year-old Dutch priest. But what stayed with him most powerfully was his experience of community. Hungry for that kind of friendly commitment that could challenge violence and injustice, Henri reflected a few years later, *Resistance that makes for peace is not so much the effort of brave and courageous individuals as the work of the community of faith.*

As a priest, Henri often heard people confide that they felt inadequate, that they were "not enough." He understood that feeling because he often felt the same way. But, he tried to explain, of course you aren't enough! None of us can ever be enough by ourselves. The truth is that we are each part of a larger body, a community. *Individual people, even the best and strongest, will soon be exhausted and discouraged, but a community of resistance can persevere even when its members have their moments of weakness and despair. Peacemaking can be a lasting work only when we live and work together.*

HENRI WAS IN CHICAGO on Thursday, April 4, 1968, when he heard that Martin Luther King Jr. was killed. The news filled Henri with a distress and horror that were amplified by the apparent detachment of his mainly White community. His anguish grew and flooded his body for days until again, he made a sudden decision:

> *There was an empty seat left on the night plane to Atlanta and I knew I had to go. During the last four days, the sorrow and sadness, the anger and madness, the pains and frustrations had crawled out of the many hidden corners of my body and spread all over like a growing disease of restlessness, tension, and bitterness. I had been fighting it all the way, but now it was clear that only his own people could cure me. Only in the anonymity of their crying, shouting, marching,*

and singing would I be able to meet the man of Selma again and find some rest.

Henri was amazed when he arrived the morning of King's funeral. *In Atlanta everything was different. A strange lightness contrasted with all my heavy feelings and expectations. No dark suits, but white dresses and colorful hats as if people were on the move to a great festival.*

He was again welcomed warmly with unexpected kindness. *Perhaps my doubt at being welcome at the funeral of a Black man had made me apprehensive. But there were only friendly questions: "Do you need any help? Transportation, breakfast, a place to stay?"*

The funeral procession was, Henri realized, Martin Luther King Jr.'s last march and everybody knew it. *But there was something strange about his last march, something new. There was no fear. There were no angry people on the sidewalks ready to throw stones. . . . When I looked back over the mile of people behind me, I had the feeling that there was no end to this victory march, no end to the stream of people singing the same song again and again. "We shall overcome, we are not afraid, Black and White together."*

The funeral procession flowed into the quiet gardens of Morehouse Seminary, and Henri collapsed onto the grass, too exhausted to watch the speeches or songs on the stage. It was too much to absorb.

Sitting on the ground surrounded by the countless people standing around me, I felt safe and protected. A Black man smiled at me when I woke up from a deep sleep. I felt exhausted, hungry, and heavy. But a strange satisfaction went through my body. This was where I wanted to be: hidden, anonymous, surrounded by Black people. It had been a long, restless trip since that Thursday night. Nervous, frantic, yearning, filled with grief and frustration. It had led me to

the green lawns of Morehouse College. And here I rested, carried by
people who kept on singing and praying.

·····•

NOW DECADES LATER, EXHAUSTED, immobilized, and waiting for the
stretcher, Henri wonders why remembering his early days with the
Rodleighs has connected in his imagination with those extraordinary
long-ago days in Alabama and Georgia. Maybe his restless body holds
memories. Maybe he is trying to figure out the paths in his life that
brought him to be so profoundly affected by the Flying Rodleighs.
Points when he discovered something about his own limitations, but
even more profoundly, saw his deepest desires for community and
beauty embodied, in a funeral procession in Atlanta, and flying above
him in Freiburg.

> *You know in this world where there is so much division, where*
> *there is so much separation, and so much violence, the Rodleighs in*
> *a way are peacemakers. They create community. They create some-*
> *thing that the world so badly needs. Who doesn't desire friendship?*
> *Who doesn't desire belonging? Who doesn't desire to laugh? Who*
> *doesn't desire to be free? Who doesn't need discipline? Who doesn't*
> *need a sense of togetherness?*

> *You know, it's all there in one act—what life is all about, what the*
> *world is all about.*

12

At the end of the week when Henri met the Flying Rodleighs, they packed swiftly and Henri waved sadly as their vehicles pulled one by one out of the Freiburg fairgrounds. He wanted to be part of their procession. He felt bereft. But just five years earlier, Henri himself had led a convoy of trucks and trailers. It was the autumn of 1986. He was not part of a traveling circus, though the event was a bit over-the-top. After a year living with people with intellectual disabilities at a L'Arche community in France, he was moving everything he owned from Boston to L'Arche Daybreak in Canada, accompanied by a troupe of friends driving a variety of vehicles.

His Harvard companions were curious and a bit skeptical. Their academic friend was choosing to live with people who didn't know who he was, would never read any of his books, who were not impressed with his credentials or history. It was hard to see how this ambitious and impatient former professor would fit. But they also knew him as someone with a remarkable ability to build and nurture community. They loved him and the vibrant community he had gathered around him during his years in Boston. Those years had left him adrift and depressed, however, and they hoped this brave new experiment might help their friend find a deeper sense of home.

As they drove up Yonge Street north of Toronto, past ugly strip malls, used car dealerships, and an astonishing number of very Canadian donut shops, his friends wondered how this was going to work out for Henri, who loved beauty, historic architecture, and culture.

One by one, Henri's convoy turned through the split-rail fencing onto the gravel laneway of the L'Arche Daybreak farm property, a big old redbrick former convent to their right and a green barn and farm fields ahead.

On the welcoming end, there was also some bewilderment. Long-time community member Sue Mosteller had welcomed many people to Daybreak, people with and without intellectual disabilities. Most assistants came wearing jeans, carrying a backpack. Henri arrived in a parade of vehicles. The last to pull into the driveway was an enormous moving van. Over the next weeks, Sue watched as the whirlwind of Henri's energy and fame shook the quiet community.

But as his friends unloaded his many boxes of books, Henri was confident that the move to L'Arche Daybreak made sense. His physical experiences of solidarity, from Selma to Latin America to L'Arche in France, had quickened in him a yearning and vision that he had carried for decades.

Ready to serve the Daybreak community's spiritual life as a priest, Henri was surprised when he arrived to be asked to live in a house with people with intellectual disabilities and their assistants. Even more jarring for Henri was that he was expected to work as a regular house assistant.

I was told that L'Arche's mission was to "live with" core members, so I embarked on my new life with all the people in the New House. Manual work, cooking, and housekeeping skills were alien to me. I had been teaching for twenty years at universities in Holland and the United States, and during this time I had never given much attention to creating a home nor had I been close to people with disabilities. In my family and among my friends, I had earned a reputation for being impractical.

A few months into this new life, early in 1987, Henri had a chance to describe his household to an audience back at Harvard:

I live in a house with six handicapped people and four assistants. None of the assistants is specially trained to work with people with a mental handicap, but we receive all the help we need from doctors, psychiatrists, behavioral management people, social workers, and psychotherapists in town. When there are no special crises, we live together as a family, gradually forgetting who is handicapped and who is not. We are simply John, Bill, Trevor, Raymond, Adam, Rose, Steve, Jane, Naomi, and Henri. We all have our gifts, our struggles, our strengths and weaknesses. We eat together, play together, pray together, and go out together. We all have our own preferences in terms of work, food, and movies, and we all have our problems in getting along with someone in the house, whether handicapped or not. We laugh a lot. We cry a lot too. Sometimes both at the same time.

Every morning when I say, "Good morning, Raymond," he says, "I am not awake yet. Saying good morning to everyone each day is unreal." Christmas Eve Trevor wrapped marshmallows in silver paper as peace gifts for everyone and at Christmas dinner he climbed on a chair, lifted his glass, and said, "Ladies and gentlemen, this is not a celebration, this is Christmas." When one of the men speaking on the phone was bothered by the cigarette smoke of an assistant, he yelled angrily, "Stop smoking; I can't hear." And every guest who comes for dinner is received by Bill with the question, "Hey, how do you keep a turkey in suspense?" When the newcomer confesses igno-rance, Bill, with a big grin on his face, says, "I'll tell you tomorrow."

Despite the moments of hilarity, adjusting to this new life was hard for Henri and for everyone around him. He was beyond impractical. His companions were amazed at his incompetence. Henri asked for help making tea, constructing a sandwich, and doing laundry. No one could understand how this engaging and caring man had survived for so long with such pitiful life skills. He felt disoriented and edgy, relaxed only when he could escape to his office to write and answer letters. Gradually, very slowly, Henri began to find a sense of belong-ing through Bill Van Buren, who was a founding member of L'Arche Daybreak in 1969.

During the past few months I have developed a friendship with one of the handicapped men in my house. His name is Bill. At first he seemed simply interested in the many little things I would do for him. And he used me well. Intuitively he knew about my guilt-ridden desire to help and he let me help him as much as possible. He let me pay for his beer, wash his dishes, and clean his room, even though he himself could do all those things pretty well. I certainly didn't feel at home with him.

But as the months went by and we came to experience many joys and pains together, something started to change. One morning he gave me a generous hug. One afternoon he proudly took me out for a beer and paid for it himself, and on my birthday he bought me a lovely gift. During dinner he wanted to sit close to me and during Mass his joking interruptions of my homily were replaced by heartfelt words of love and concern. Thus we were becoming friends.

·····•

DENNIE CHECKS THE OXYGEN levels on Henri's finger monitor and hides his concern. He tries to encourage Henri. "Things are moving along well. The fire department trucks are on their way. They will be here in a few minutes. We just have to wait. The medication I am giving you should help soon and your body will be able to relax."

Henri is not listening. He is remembering Adam.

·····•

Adam is the weakest person of our family. He is a twenty-five-year-old man who cannot speak, cannot dress or undress himself, cannot walk alone or eat without much help. He does not cry, or laugh, and only occasionally makes eye contact. His back is distorted and his arm and leg movements are very twisted. He suffers from severe epilepsy and, not withstanding heavy medications, there are few days without grand mal seizures. Sometimes, as he grows suddenly rigid, he utters a howling groan, and on a few occasions I have seen a big tear coming down his cheek.

Although Henri had spent time in L'Arche in France, he had not worked directly with any of the people with disabilities. He was quite afraid to enter this unfamiliar world. This fear did not lessen when he was asked to work directly with Adam.

I was aghast! I simply didn't think I could do this. "What if he falls? How do I support him as he walks? What if I hurt him and he cannot even tell me? What if he has a seizure? What if I make his bath too hot or too cold? What if I cut him? I do not even know how to dress him! So many things can go wrong. Besides, I don't know the man. I'm not a nurse. I have no training in this kind of thing!" Some of these many objections I voiced; most of them I just thought. But the answer was clear, firm, and reassuring: "You can do it. First of all, we will help you and give you plenty of time until you feel comfortable. . . . You'll learn the routine, and you will get to know Adam and he will get to know you."

So I began with fear and trembling. I still remember those first days. Even with the support of other assistants, I was afraid walking into Adam's room and waking up this stranger. His heavy breathing and restless hand movements made me very self-conscious. I didn't know him. I didn't know what he expected of me. I didn't want to upset him. And in front of the others, I didn't want to make a fool of myself. I didn't want to be laughed at. I didn't want to be a source of embarrassment.

A few months later, Henri was describing the routine to his Harvard audience:

It takes me about an hour and a half to wake Adam up, give him his medication, undress him, carry him into his bath, wash him, shave him, clean his teeth, dress him, walk him to the kitchen, give him his breakfast, put him in his wheelchair, and bring him to the place where he spends most of the day with different therapeutic exercises. When a grand mal seizure occurs during this sequence of activities, much more time is needed, and often he has to return to sleep to regain some of the energy spent during such a seizure.

In those early days Henri saw Adam as someone who was very different. Adam did not talk, so Henri did not imagine that they could ever communicate. The relationship was very physical. When Henri walked with Adam,

I had to get behind him and support him with my body. I worried constantly that he would trip on my feet, fall and hurt himself. I also was conscious that he could have a grand mal seizure at any moment: sitting in the bathtub, on the toilet, eating his breakfast, resting, walking, or being shaved.

At first I had to keep asking myself and others, "Why have you asked me to do this? Why did I say yes? What am I doing here? Who is the stranger who is demanding a big chunk of my time each day? Why should I, the least capable of all the people in the house, be asked to take care of Adam and not of someone whose needs are a bit less?" The answer was always the same: "So you can get to know Adam." Now, that was a puzzle for me. Adam often looked at me and followed me with his eyes, but he did not speak or respond to anything I asked him.

Gradually, very gradually, things started to change. My whole life had been shaped by words, ideas, books, and encyclopedias. But now my priorities were shifting. What was becoming important for

me was Adam and our privileged time together when he offered me his body in total vulnerability, when he gave me himself, to be undressed, bathed, dressed, fed, and walked from place to place. Being close to Adam's body brought me closer to Adam. I was slowly getting to know him.

13

While Dennie has been attending to Henri, the ambulance driver has gathered Henri's suitcases and carry-on bag. He has found Henri's medication, but he hasn't yet found a toothbrush or other toiletries. Dennie leans close to Henri to get his attention. "We can take one bag with us to the hospital now. Is everything you need for a night or two in your carry-on bag?"

Henri's fuzzy brain tries to decide. He won't need his notes about Rembrandt in the hospital, nor his suit. The brightly colored stole from Latin America that he wears to say Mass is in his carry-on, as well as some wafers, a small chalice for wine, a Bible, and his daily book of morning and evening prayers. Yes, that is all I need, he nods.

·••••

HENRI'S MIND FLOATS, WANDERING from the trapeze and the Rodleighs to his Daybreak community. *When I think about Circus Barum and Daybreak, I think of two international communities of people who want to bring joy and peace to the world. The handicapped people at Daybreak and the talented artists of Circus Barum have much more in common than it would seem at first glance.*

But then why, Henri wonders, when he had moved to Daybreak and built a friendship with Bill and Adam and his new household, did he have a complete emotional breakdown in 1987?

His commitment for peace and social change had not diminished, and his living situation and work had refocused in a way that he had hungered for since Selma, moving from an *issue-oriented life* to a *person-oriented life*. And yet it nearly destroyed him.

That really was the problem. He had oriented his life around others, what they thought of him, how they responded. As a trained psychologist as well as a priest, Henri was aware of his insecurities. Close friendships had collapsed under the weight of his hopes and expectations before.

Possibly what changed at Daybreak was that he felt supported enough to finally risk facing this side of himself in a way that was impossible before. Did his new community trigger all his anguish? No, like a trapeze act, Daybreak and his new friends gave him a place where he could finally fall. And unexpectedly, a key part of that safety net was Adam.

I began to realize that the gentle safety of the New House was weakening many of the defenses I had created around my inner handicaps. In this loving, caring milieu, without competition, one-upmanship, and great pressure to distinguish myself, I experienced what I had not been able to see or experience before. I was faced with a very insecure, needy and fragile person: myself. Looking out from this vantage point I saw Adam as the strong one. He was always there, quiet, peaceful, and inwardly steady. Adam, Rosie, Michael, John, and Roy—they all showed themselves to me as the solid core of our community.

Toward the end of 1987 I realized that I was headed for a crisis. I wasn't sleeping well and I was preoccupied by a friendship that had seemed life-giving but had gradually become suffocating for me. It was as if the planks that had covered my emotional abyss had been taken away and I was looking into a canyon full of wild animals waiting to devour me. I found myself overwhelmed by intense feelings of abandonment, rejection, neediness, dependence, despair. Here I was in the most peaceful house, with the most peaceful people but raging inside myself.

Henri's friend Sue and others were deeply worried. Henri was barely holding himself together during the day, and at night in the safety of the small chapel in Daybreak's retreat house where Sue lived, she could hear Henri's anguished cries. Sometimes she would go sit with him as he writhed in physical agony.

I spoke to a few members of my community, at first obliquely but then quite openly and directly. I soon found myself speaking to a psychiatrist. Everyone said the same thing: "It is time for you to face your demons. It is time to bind your own wounds, to let others care for you."

It was a very humbling proposal. I had to leave the New House and the community for a place where I could live through my anguish in the hope of finding new strength and new peace. What did it all mean? I didn't know. I had come to live in community and to care for Adam. Now I had to leave Adam to others and fully acknowledge my own disabilities.

For years, Henri had been moved by the Bible story of Jesus's baptism, when a voice from heaven was heard identifying God's pleasure in Jesus as God's beloved child. For Henri, it was a voice he longed to hear personally: unconditional divine love affirming him.

I was going through the deep human struggle to believe in my belovedness even when I had nothing to be proud of. Yes, I had left the university with its prestige, but this life gave me satisfaction and even brought me admiration. Yes, I was considered a good, even a noble person because I was helping the poor! But now that the last crutch had been taken away, I was challenged to believe that even when I had nothing to show for myself, I was still God's beloved son.

As I lived through this emotional ordeal I realized that I was becoming like Adam. He had nothing to be proud of. Neither had I. He was completely empty. So was I. He needed full-time attention. So did I.

I found myself resisting this "becoming like Adam." I did not want to be dependent and weak. I did not want to be so needy. Somewhere, though, I recognized that Adam's way, the way of radical vulnerability, was also the way of Jesus.

During the months that I spent away from L'Arche Daybreak I was able—with much guidance—to hear a soft and gentle inner voice saying, "You are my beloved child, on you my favor rests." For a long time I distrusted the voice. I kept saying to myself, "It is a lie. I know the truth. There is nothing in me worth loving." But my guides were there, encouraging me to listen to that voice and let it become stronger.

Henri committed himself to six months of intensive psychological and spiritual accompaniment far from L'Arche Daybreak. Sue covered his pastoral ministry at Daybreak, spoke on the phone with him daily, and visited him. Through therapy, Henri began to understand more of his compulsion to get right into the lives of others. He wrote, *When you find yourself curious about the lives of people you are with or filled with desires to possess them in one way or another, your body has not yet come fully home.*

He began fumbling toward a new way of thinking about what he wanted to articulate as a writer, priest, and speaker. *A new spirituality is being born in you. Not body denying or body indulging but truly incarnational.* But opening himself to something new implied changes. *You will discover that many other spiritualities you have admired and tried to practice no longer fit your unique call.*

By July 1988, Henri was still fragile but he returned to the Daybreak community, where he was welcomed home. He now lived in the community retreat house, a four-bedroom family home that had been built in the early years of Daybreak. The community's small chapel was in the converted basement. The Daybreak woodworking shop had already built tall wall-to-wall bookshelves in the living room to make Henri's library available to everyone.

Sue and he would share the house and together they would care for Daybreak's spiritual needs. Henri occupied one of the small bedrooms, but he had a private phone line installed. He shared a bathroom with whichever random retreatants were staying in the house. Henri's new home was modest and he would have very little privacy, but he could welcome friends and community members. He liked living simply.

14

As Rodleigh drove away from Freiburg in 1991 in the convoy of circus trailers, he kept thinking about the new friend who had become so dear in just a week. Henri's gentle and friendly way of getting to know each of them was unusual—bold, yet sincere and attentive.

"We have a letter from Henri!" Rodleigh announced to Jennie about five weeks later. They were especially touched to read that Henri had felt completely welcome with the troupe. Really, thought Rodleigh, it hadn't been a big deal. In fact, it took relatively little effort to make Henri feel at ease. Henri was eager to be pleased, and each member of the Flying Rodleigh troupe genuinely liked him.

When Rodleigh and Karlene's mother died suddenly a few months later, Henri's sensitive and supportive letters meant a great deal to the grieving troupe members. They later told Henri about their struggle to perform immediately after hearing of their mother's death. "The way we got around it—I found out later that my sister and I both had the same feeling—was that we were doing our performance for our mother," Rodleigh told Henri. "Wherever she was, the feeling that I had was that it was a special moment, a special time."

By the end of the summer, Henri asked if he could visit them again. Everyone was pleased. Jon offered to host him in his new trailer, and Jennie prepared to feed Henri's voracious appetite.

After Circus Barum had left Freiburg and I had returned to Toronto, where I live in the L'Arche Daybreak community, I kept in touch with the Flying Rodleighs through letters. In November 1991—at their invitation—I returned to Germany to spend a week with them on their travels from town to town.

Henri took a taxi from the train station to join them on November 11 in Korbach, Germany, physically tired but as bright-eyed and excited as a child in a toy shop.

"That was wonderful!" were Henri's delighted first words following the afternoon performance just hours after he arrived. He tried to nap, but was too excited to sleep and joined Rodleigh and Jennie for supper.

"I'd forgotten how much he can eat!" Jennie laughed to Rodleigh.

After supper, despite his recent transatlantic flight, Henri watched their evening show as well. He was especially glad that he stayed awake, because Jon and Joe got into an argument during the evening's after-show debriefing. The troupe was embarrassed to deal with it in Henri's presence, but he loved it. He was delighted to see that the Flying Rodleighs were human and made mistakes and had to work on their relationships just like everyone else.

Sharing those intimate moments of emotional struggle, problem-solving, and commitment to a common purpose made Henri feel more involved, Rodleigh realized. Henri was almost imperceptibly becoming part of their family.

Hosting Henri turned out to be risky. One day the whole troupe went to get work visas at the Italian consulate, sixty miles away. Henri stayed in Jon's new trailer watching circus videos. When the troupe arrived back, he was on his knees in front of the TV, so entranced that he had forgotten the kettle that he had begun heating on the gas stove. The enamel exterior was charred black. Jon was not impressed, but as they got to know Henri better, they were just relieved that he hadn't burned down the whole trailer. Jennie and Rodleigh soon discovered that even drying the dishes was too dangerous for their awkward and overly enthusiastic friend, and they tactfully declined his further assistance.

They loved his presence, however. He was not just immersed in his subject, Rodleigh observed, but wallowing in it. They were tickled to see him sprawled across Jon's couch, expressing his thoughts with flamboyant hand gestures and an air of total belonging and contentment. He was especially intrigued by their perfectionism, their complete concentration, as well as the self-confidence and teamwork required to perform their ten-minute act. He often asked how they focused so completely, how they were able to put aside all the other things going through their minds, and Rodleigh could only say discipline and practice.

In mid-November, Henri interviewed each member of the troupe. He ended with Rodleigh, delving into Rodleigh's childhood, his family and religious background, his relationships, and his development as a creative artist. The three-hour interview ended abruptly as Henri bolted away to catch his train, and Rodleigh and Jennie found their trailer felt quite empty that afternoon after the show. Henri was eccentric and peculiar, but very lovable. By that evening, they were already missing him. He brought a different level of awareness to their lives, a deeper sense of themselves as a community, perhaps because of his own rootedness in community life.

> *During that week the idea grew in me to write a book—maybe even a novel?—about this remarkable group. They gladly gave me the freedom to interview them and write about them in any way I chose. Living with them for a week opened my eyes and heart to a new world of art, community, and friendship.*

Back in Canada soon afterward, Henri announced his latest book idea to his friends Bart and Patricia Gavigan. Writers, filmmakers, and directors of a Christian ecumenical community and center in England, they had faithfully helped him through the early and later stages of his breakdown in 1987. Now they were in Toronto showing their new film *Zabelka: The Reluctant Prophet,* and Henri joined their workshop on nonviolence. That evening, he gave a keynote talk to thousands of Catholic school teachers, but by the time they got to their car in the underground parking garage he was bursting to tell them about a totally different kind of project.

"I feel like I am now at a crucial crossroads as a writer," he explained. "I want to write for a secular audience this time."

Bart groaned and rolled his eyes. Henri had been saying this for years.

But this time Henri had a new kind of project in mind. "I want my next book to be about the flying trapeze! I think it is such a good story that it will be a kind of cross-over book for me."

He paused. Now he had Bart's and Patricia's full attention, so Henri ventured an even deeper intuition: "I have never before attempted a book like this, but I believe this could be the most important thing I ever write. What do you think?"

"Go for it!" said his friends. Then lightheartedly picking up his own imagery for his new vision, they added, "Try a triple somersault!"

III

Teamwork

15

"Here's what will happen next," Dennie says to Henri. "The fire department is sending two trucks. The truck with the aerial lift is a supporting unit, so it will come with a standard pumper truck. The pumper will have a crew of six, including the captain. He will coordinate the whole team, both the two in the aerial truck and the six men in his pumper truck. Most of them will come upstairs with the stretcher, so your room will feel a bit full, but everyone has a role. You will see that it is good to have many hands available."

I hope all those people know how to work well together, thinks Henri. He wonders if they like each other. The anticipated large crew reminds him of his very first impressions of the Flying Rodleighs, which he dictated onto a tape the week he first met them.

•••••

Karlene was making these tapes with her camera and I was standing beside her. They were trying to do something new, and it was absolutely fascinating to see because it was very difficult and they couldn't do it. Every time they made that move either Rod was too late in arriving or Joe was too early in coming or Jon Griggs was too late in letting Rod go, or similar various little mistakes, denying them success or consistency. They couldn't figure it out. Rod wasn't caught by Joe and came down in the net. And that's not a small thing coming down in the net, to fall all the way from the top to the bottom. Falling in the net is really dangerous. It looks rather easy, but you can really hurt yourself, and they all suffer from painful shoulders, stiff necks, and all that.

But one of the things I saw was that these people really work well together. Rod was clearly the one who was the leader. Everybody listened very carefully to him. They are willing to follow his instructions, and there was a kind of gentleness about it.

And then they did some new practices with Rod and Jennie together on the Russian swing. This is a sort of big double-decker swing and they can give it an enormous amount of momentum by building the swing together. They take off from that swing and get propelled all the way to the top to Jon Griggs and he then throws them all the way to Joe, or they go right up into the middle of the air and mount to stands high up with Jon. It is just incredible.

On Friday I went to the practice again. They did the same thing—it went wrong—then it went well, and they tried all over again. They didn't practice very long and one of the reasons was that it was terribly cold. I realized how sensitive they are about health things because as soon as one of them gets sick or one of them is not able to do it, they can't do the act, and there are no replacements. So here are five people and they all have to be there. They all have to be healthy and in good shape.

And it has to be a good atmosphere to be successful. They had a flyer who was cocky and didn't want to help out with simple things. It isn't easy when one of them is not really connected and doesn't fit. So that's another aspect of the whole thing—how they work together, practice together, and so on. They really are sensitive to each other's needs.

•••••

THE MEDICATION IN THE IV must be working, Henri observes with relief. Dennie had said that it was a combination of two drugs. It could lower your blood pressure even further, Dennie had warned, so do not try to get up. Henri is not even tempted. Not now. He is remembering being inside an egg.

•••••

IN THE MONTHS AFTER Henri returned from his week traveling with the Flying Rodleighs, two big events for him happened at L'Arche Daybreak.

The first was in December 1991. Some of Henri's friends came for a discernment process to help Henri and Daybreak to reflect back over his five years at Daybreak and consider his future. For days, the community reminisced about Henri. Uproarious and touching and appreciative and annoying stories were told around dinner tables. As the three visitors listened to community members reflect on Henri's half decade, it became clear that Henri needed help to balance his community life with time away from the community to write.

The discernment process culminated in an evening event with invited dignitaries from three Christian churches: Catholic, Anglican, and the United Church of Canada. Alongside a more serious evaluation of Henri's contributions and challenges through his first five years at Daybreak, community members presented ridiculous songs and skits about Henri, such as a version of "The Man on the Flying Trapeze" with the lyrics adjusted to acknowledge Henri's infatuation with the Flying Rodleighs and his frequent flights around the world. Even though some of the skits were rather pointed, Henri did not feel hurt. "I didn't know that you knew me so well," he marveled afterward.

In January, L'Arche Daybreak threw him a big circus-themed sixtieth birthday party in the community meeting hall. Hung from the ceiling and along the walls were enormous homemade banners with exuberant paintings depicting clowns and trapeze artists. The guests were treated to skits, stories, songs, speeches, and general absurdity.

The highlight was when Robert Morgan, a long-term friend of L'Arche and of Henri's, invited Henri to be reborn as a baby clown. By then Henri had been softened up with lots of hilarious and affectionate attention. He was in his element. Without hesitation, he leapt to his feet to join Robert in the middle of the community gathering.

An actor, playwright, and professional clown himself, Robert carefully dressed Henri as a clown, layering over his clothes a baggy, shiny top, then an extravagant ruffled collar. Henri pulled a pair of calf-length pantaloons over his dress pants and shoes, then Robert added a final touch: a snug red beanie cap that came down over his ears. To the delight of his assembled guests, the distinguished author and former professor now looked very silly. He handed his glasses to one of the viewers and entered wholeheartedly into the transformation, beaming with anticipation.

Robert next produced a large white cloth sack decorated with a few bright swatches of fabric, and announced that this was a clown egg. He explained to Henri what would happen next.

Now to begin your life as a clown you have to go right back to the very beginning. This is a clown egg. . . . A little baby clown will come out of this egg. So you are going to come inside this. You have to realize that when you're in there—you know that Bible passage about being knitted in your mother's womb—that's what's going to happen to you inside this egg. You're going to be knitted together into a baby clown and you'll feel at some point that your body begins to work a little bit in there.

You know babies, when they're ready to come out, they have to come out. When you're ready, when you feel knitted together, what you can do is come out. Come out of the egg. But remember, you've never breathed, you've never even taken a breath. So you have to take your first breath. You can feel your body for the first time. You've never felt the air on your face. You've never opened your eyes to the light. You don't know what your hand is. You don't know a thing about your body. In fact, you don't know anything about anything! Isn't it wonderful being sixty?

Henri climbed into the cloth egg, and Robert dragged the bundle to the middle of the room and left it. Everyone watched eagerly.

Nothing happened for a while. Then, slowly, the sack began to twitch. It rolled over a few times. It wriggled, expanding and contracting. Finally, out of the opening emerged—a bare foot! A hairy calf with the cuff of the pantaloon at the knee! The room rocked with laughter, and the shy leg retreated back into the egg.

Moments later, it reappeared, cautiously, followed by the other leg. The two bare legs waved in the air, stretching their toes, exploring.

The sack rolled over again, and Henri's face emerged, wide-eyed, curious. With just his feet and head showing, he rolled onto his back, then reached up to grab his toes, just like a baby. He tried to put his toes into his mouth.

The baby clown sat up and looked around, blinking in newborn confusion. Gradually, with the assistance of some of his friends, mainly those with intellectual disabilities and the many children led by Robert, he gingerly rose to his feet, and found out how his arms worked. Imitating Robert, he discovered his voice, practicing first simple vowels then syllables as everyone present howled with laughter. With his arm around Henri's shoulders, Robert moved his attention beyond the discovery of his own body and introduced him to the assembled company, "your family."

"They love you, Henri," he explained, "and you will find that you love them, too."

The rebirth ended with Robert singing Bob Dylan's "Forever Young." Everyone who knew the words joined in: "May you always do for others, and let others do for you. May you build a ladder to the stars, and climb on every rung. . . ."

16

Yes, remembers Henri, that was the year he became so much younger, the year he turned sixty. He rediscovered his body, letting it be reborn from the clown egg into his loving and supportive community. He gave himself fully to the moment, open to transformation. Meeting the Flying Rodleighs the previous spring, he had felt like an infatuated adolescent. They gave him a whole new way to imagine what it might be to "climb on every rung." It was an unexpected ladder up to a new platform, but it felt risky. After all, every time the Rodleighs climbed, they knew they might fall. He could not get his new friends out of his mind.

His response to the Rodleighs' performance had been very physical, but his previous books had been about inward, spiritual movements and choices. He did not know how to put his experience into words. In fact, he felt what he termed *a certain inner resistance.* He decided to go to England to participate in a writing workshop led by Bart and Patricia Gavigan.

"What is the risk?" was a key question in the Gavigans' film-writing workshop in February 1992, and the question gripped Henri's imagination. *What is the risk?* he wrote in his notebook, thinking about his book about the Flying Rodleighs, and began making a list beginning simply with *time.* He continued with *security,* but also noted an *enigma: totally confident but do not know why.* It was like *traveling without maps, where your own map doesn't take you.* Henri found himself groping for a route beyond his own comfort zone, wondering how to explain his experience of the Flying Rodleighs on a *psychological-emotional level.*

What is this about? he wrote, and suggested some possible answers to himself: *Is this just an adolescent memory, just living out your fantasy?* There was clearly *sexual energy, with its invitation to fantasy,* and *that is in everyone.*

But Henri did not want to limit the power of the trapeze image. To make the experience accessible to all his readers, Henri wanted to identify *another reality* that would *desexualize* his experience.

Either way he saw a risk. He could explore his physical response to the trapeze act, or shift his attention to the safer *spiritual dimension,* which he named as *no more or less important than anything else.*

The problem, he realized, was that he wanted to write *not a spiritual book, but a book about life, examining life on all levels and letting them fall in their own place.* That meant trying to integrate the physical experience into a story about all of life. He had never before attempted to write anything like it.

YOUR journey has to be as vital as the circus story, wrote Henri, recalling Bart's encouragement. *Create curiosity, surprise people occasionally. Can you create apprehension? Even a feeling of foreboding? What is the end of the story? What is the climax?*

These were central questions to any good story, Henri realized. He had imagined that the climax had something to do with bringing together the world of the circus and the world of community with handicapped people. One of the first things that struck him about the Flying Rodleighs was the fun they had, the way they smiled at each other as they performed, the way they radiated a joyful spirit of community.

So when those two worlds of L'Arche and the trapeze meet, he thought, they could bring the reader into a kind of *total absorption, total delight.*

Working with Bart, Henri's own ideas, fantasies, and connections between communities seemed like a dramatic story of delight, risk, and surprise. But as the workshop carried on, writing from even that set of notes fell flat. He was losing the intense physical experience of seeing the Rodleighs.

HE NEEDED TO BE with them again. That spring, he initiated a daring plan to join the Flying Rodleighs' convoy for several weeks.

17

Back in Toronto, when I spoke about my experience with the Flying Rodleighs in my community, my desire to return and deepen my connection with the circus grew. Yes, I wanted to write about them, but to do that well I needed more immersion than a week would allow.

In May 1992 I flew to Amsterdam, rented a camper to have as my own little home for reading and writing, and returned to the circus. Since Rodleigh had given me their itinerary, I knew where to catch up with them. This happened to be close to the Dutch border, only one hour's drive from my father's home.

On Monday, May 4th, I arrived with my little mobile home in Geysteren—a small village in the Dutch province of Limburg—and parked in the front yard of my father's house. My father was excited about my plans, and he and a friend from the village helped me find all I needed for my camper to be self-sufficient.

R odleigh and the troupe were delighted when Henri wrote to ask if he could travel with them for two weeks. For Henri writing would be a key focus, so he eagerly packed his books about creative writing. *As I drove away from my father's home, I said to myself: "This time I will keep a diary."*

Wednesday, May 6—Emmerich

Around noon I arrived in Emmerich. It wasn't hard to find the circus since all along the road there were "Circus Barum" signs. Last night the Flying Rodleighs had arrived here from the small town of Gogh, and this morning was "build-up" time. Around noon Rodleigh, Jon, and Joe were busy setting up the riggings, while the Moroccans were finishing the work on the tents.

I am happy to be here again. Another world, so different from my Daybreak community in Toronto and yet so similar. Animal trainers, clowns, acrobats, magicians, tumblers, flyers, and catchers living in a small "village on wheels" together with musicians, stable hands, electricians, and many handymen. They come from all over the world: Germany, Russia, Hungary, Italy, Spain, France, Morocco, South Africa, and the U.S.

When he arrived in Emmerich, the three men in the troupe welcomed him warmly, and took a break from setting up the rigging to park his camper in front of Joe's truck. The circus grounds were too small for all the circus vehicles, so the trailers were parked in a row along the street.

Henri was eager to watch as they resumed their work finishing the rigging and setting up the net. Recent rains had left the ground soft, so it took several tries and extra stakes to firmly anchor the net. Henri perched on a bleacher seat and immediately started writing notes. Rodleigh cheerfully braced himself for his friend's newest round of questions. In a hurry to be ready for the afternoon show, he was surprised by the level of technical detail that Henri requested. After the evening show, when the questioning continued, Rodleigh resorted to drawing diagrams for Henri. They shared a long discussion of Henri's latest book ideas, then Rodleigh walked Henri to his camper van, knowing he was likely to become disoriented in the darkness.

Karlene's new trailer arrived the next day, and Henri sprawled contentedly on her couch, chatting companionably as she and Kail unpacked.

Thursday, May 7

I have now seen the flying trapeze act of the Flying Rodleighs four more times, and each time I am stunned by their magnificent performance in the air. Their act has not changed since November. It remains spectacular, elegant, and very artistic. It also remains dangerous! Every time they have their evaluation meeting after the act, it becomes clearer to me how much can go wrong. It is all split-second work.

After the evening show, Henri's friends checked that his camper van had enough water in its tanks and charged its batteries for the trip. Rodleigh considered how best to arrange the convoy, and decided that he would lead, followed by Jennie driving Karlene's trailer, then Henri followed by Joe, with Jon at the rear.

As they set out in the dark, Henri discovered with dismay that writing in a new way was not actually his biggest challenge: driving the large van terrified him.

Rodleigh didn't realize how anxious Henri was about driving his big vehicle at night until they stopped. Rodleigh walked over, and saw that Henri was still clutching the steering wheel with white knuckles. Rodleigh asked him if he was okay. "I have never driven anything so large before," Henri blurted out desperately, "and I have never liked driving at night, and I don't know what to do now—I can't park it." He nearly wept with relief when Rodleigh took over the wheel of the camper van and parked it for him.

Henri slept well, however, and the next morning, Rodleigh found him up early, sitting at his table enjoying the view. Rodleigh connected Henri's electricity, and was startled to find that Henri had already used up all his water. He showed Henri how to refill his tanks, and warned him to be less extravagant in his water use.

By the time Henri sat down to write his journal later that day, the terrifying drive felt like history, and his focus had returned to his connection with Rodleigh and the trapeze act itself.

Friday, May 8—Borken

Last night we drove to the next town: Borken. It was a good 90-minute ride. We arrived safely, and I was glad because driving my camper at night fills me with fear.

I asked Rodleigh if he would be willing to give me a moment-by-moment commentary on the videotape of their flying trapeze act. He invited me to his trailer and gave me a very detailed analysis of the first movement in which he does a full-twist double-layout. The whole movement lasts less than 10 seconds, but this commentary, once I had transcribed it from the tape, filled three folio pages!

Saturday, May 9

During the afternoon performance Rodleigh missed his "long jump." It was a dramatic moment to see him pass Joe's hands and drop into the net. Then he repeated the jump, and this time, to the loud applause of the audience, Joe caught him safely.

It is strange, but after having seen the flying trapeze act countless times, I am not any less nervous. To the contrary. Since I now know more about the intricacies of the act, I am more aware of how much can go wrong, and I feel more tension than last year when I first saw it. I even said to myself, "I don't want to see it again; it makes me too anxious." But I know that I will see it many more times.

After the backstage evaluation session, Joe invited me for coffee in his caravan. We talked about catching. "I knew I couldn't catch Rodleigh on the first long jump," he said. "When I saw him passing Jon, I realized he was not getting close enough for me to touch him. He was out of my reach." I asked what the problem was. "It is the coordination between Jennie and Rodleigh on the Russian swing. The way Rodleigh was boosted up by Jennie made him go too high and not far enough." I tried to get some ideas as to how much flexibility Joe had in catching Rodleigh. I was amazed to hear him describe the many adjustments he could make to get Rodleigh safely in his hands.

He explained how he could see Rodleigh coming to him. Although he didn't observe details, he could see the total form of his body and was able to reach out to him in such a way that he could make a definite miss into a possible catch. "Sometimes I have to cross my arms so that I can catch both of his wrists and turn him so that we can come straight as we swing above the apron." As he spoke, I realized how much was happening within less than a second.

Joe also explained what it means for him when Rodleigh comes late or early: "When he is late I have to slow down my swing. When he is early I have to speed it up. I usually know whether he is late or early when I see him flying past Jon. Then I know mostly what to do. But when he gets up too high and his body moves back in the direction of the pedestal, I know there is no chance of catching him. Then I just have to let him go into the net."

The more I hear about the details of this short trapeze act, the more I am aware of how long it is. I know how, in a critical moment, life can go into slow motion. People in car accidents often tell you how much they saw, thought about, and felt from the moment they lost control of the wheel until the moment they hit the tree or another car. Some people even say they saw their whole life pass by in a second.

Now I realize what Joe sees, feels, and decides within the few seconds Rodleigh flies toward him. It must be like watching a movie in slow motion. I also realize that what is true for Joe is also true for Rodleigh, Jennie, Jon, and Karlene. Their ten-minute act is a long and complicated series of maneuvers that takes many hours to describe. What the public sees is the highly compact result of many thoughts, movements, choices, adaptations, successes, and failures that only slowly become visible to a trained eye. Often, when I join them after the act and congratulate them on their success—success for me means that nobody fell into the net during the act—they end up listing all their mistakes. In the beginning I didn't notice any of these "mistakes" and even now I mostly miss them.

The flying trapeze is a microcosm, even though it looks like a broad and free movement of flying and catching. Being with the Rodleighs is like being invited by a biologist to look through a microscope and become aware that a lot more is happening on my thumb than my naked eye can see.

JENNIE WELCOMED HENRI WARMLY when he dropped by late that afternoon. "I want to ask Rodleigh to check my description of the full-twist double-layout routine," he explained.

Jennie persuaded Henri to settle in and discuss the act with her. She knew that Rodleigh would be in no mood for a discussion. He was out trying to fix the heating system of the secondhand Mercedes-Benz that he purchased the day before. Hopefully the new, more spacious trailer for Karlene would have no problems. Henri happily accepted a cup of tea and tucked into Jennie's plate of cookies.

I asked Jennie to tell me more about boosting Rodleigh for the long jump. She gladly explained: "It requires real coordination. I have to time Rodleigh's leaving. I say: 'Ready . . . go.' But many things can go wrong. I can say 'go' too early or too late. Rodleigh can leave too early or too late. Since I weigh less than Rodleigh, I really depend on the momentum of the Russian swing and can't put my body weight behind it if I'm out of time with him."

Speaking about her adjustments, Jennie said: "When Rodleigh leaves too early, he will travel too long and end up too close to Joe. When he leaves too late, he goes too high up and does not come close enough to Joe. I have to make the corrections. When I see him leaving too late, I have to push harder; when I notice him leaving too early, I have to hold back." Her explanation puzzled me greatly. "How can your 'pushing' harder make any difference when Rodleigh leaves too late?" I asked, thinking that leaving means being away from the swing. "Well," Jenny said, "when Rodleigh leaves too late I see his body moving toward the cut-off too late. I then realize that I have to give him an extra boost."

That afternoon, Rodleigh had started the act feeling frustrated that the car he had just purchased already needed repairs. When he missed his long jump, the most dramatic part of their act, he felt his mood sink. It was his own fault, an obvious failure of concentration. He really did not feel like discussing it with anyone, especially not with Henri, but neither did he want to take his ill humor out on Henri, so he pushed himself to answer Henri's questions.

To his surprise, he felt better after talking with Henri about it. Henri had that effect, Rodleigh realized, not just for him but on every member of the troupe. Since Henri was not expecting perfection from people, he accepted human failure more easily than did Rodleigh.

The evening show of the Flying Rodleighs was stunning. Everything went smoothly—what a joy to see, what beauty and what grace! It was electrifying. The public applauded and stamped their feet with wild enthusiasm.

18

Saturday, May 9 evening

After the intermission I returned to the tent to see the Russian trio, Kaminski. They work on the Russian bar, three pole-vaulting poles taped together. The trio consists of two men and a woman. The men hold the bar on their shoulders while the woman leaps from the bar or pole somersaulting and twisting. The whole breathtaking act is done in a ballet-like fashion with riveting music. They are true disciples of the famous Moscow school. Rodleigh told me that it had taken them many years to train for this athletic routine, and they would do nothing else but this act in its present form for the rest of their professional careers. This really brought home to me the complication of artistic specialization. What they did was perfect, but it would never be different—a little like a pianist who can play one Chopin waltz perfectly but will never play anything else!

Karlene celebrated her new trailer with a little housewarming party that evening and no one was surprised when Henri was the first to arrive for more tea and biscuits.

Henri busily observed everything he could about the Flying Rodleighs, and Rodleigh couldn't help watching Henri with equal attention. After three days, Henri looked like he had been with them for years. Rodleigh noticed with amusement that he walked around the circus grounds with what Rodleigh recognized as his air of confidence, but what would likely appear to others like a confused lost child.

At least once a day, Rodleigh would go through a video of the day's performance with Henri and recount in minute detail what each person was doing and how it felt. Henri was mesmerized watching it in slow motion, marveling at how the human body could perform such a dance in the air. Day by day, he learned the new language of the trapeze.

As well as the physical discipline, he was fascinated by the mental focus required. As Rodleigh explained: "Once you're on that pedestal and once you're on the catch bar, you cannot think about anything else that is happening in your life at that time."

Beyond the obvious physical and mental challenges of the trapeze act, the troupe also had to face emotional upheavals without letting those affect their performance. Often he asked the Rodleighs about their feelings and about their interaction with each other.

Rodleigh enjoyed what he called these "psychological conversations" with Henri. As leader, he had to initiate discussions of any mistakes after each act.

"I have to be able to let them each know their mistake is okay," Rodleigh said to Henri. "I can't hide my disappointment in the overall performance that we did. But I cannot come back and say, 'Why did you do this? It's your fault. Why didn't you concentrate?' That's not going to instill any confidence in them for the next performance. I have to provide leadership so that the next time they go up they can feel, 'All right, now I'm going to do it' because each one has their own pride."

"What you say is incredibly important for life, not just for the trapeze," responded Henri. *"Your willingness not to accuse first, not to point your finger and say, 'You did something wrong' but simply to take the reality and continue to say to people, 'I will be with you, and you will do it well the next time.' That's a wonderful kind of discipline."*

Henri began to list various facets of Rodleigh's position in the troupe. "Your role is very complicated!" Henri said. "Everyone relies on you for their emotional strength and willpower. As troupe leader, you have to create peace when there is discord, make important decisions for the other troupe members, and offer concern and support for each in their personal lives."

Rodleigh felt his body growing tense. He had not thought about his role in that way before, and the pressure of all these new responsibilities weighed heavily. But then he realized that nothing had changed. Henri had just helped him to name the many roles that he was already carrying. He shifted his shoulders and relaxed.

Their conversations gave Rodleigh insight into both the lives of his troupe and Henri himself. He appreciated the way that Henri thought of them not only as artists but also as people.

Henri was pleased with Rodleigh's explanations, repeating them over again, putting them into his own words, finding parallels and similarities to his own life.

Sunday, May 10

This morning I went to a Catholic church in town, a two-minute walk from the circus entrance. There were a lot of church bells ringing through the air—as if they were competing with one another—but when I entered the church all was harmony and peace. By the time Mass began, the church was practically full. The celebration was carefully structured. The priest presided with great devotion, gave a well-prepared homily, and said the eucharistic prayer with conviction and clarity.

As in most German churches, there was much order and little intimacy. People scarcely greeted each other, and the sign of peace was omitted. I realized how similar, yet how different, this celebration was compared to my Daybreak celebrations. I felt deeply grateful to hear God's Word and to receive God's gifts, but also somewhat lost in this big church and its formal liturgy. Everything was so familiar yet so distant and strange.

No one from the circus was there. The circus tent and the church, standing a few hundred feet apart, are two completely separate worlds. For me, however, they are very connected, but no one seems to see this. Aren't they both trying to lift up the human spirit and help people look beyond the boundaries of their daily lives? And aren't they both, at the same time, in constant peril of becoming places for lifeless routines that have lost their vitality and transcending power?

I tried to stay a little longer in the church after most of the people had left. But I couldn't pray. I felt lost in this vast space in which everything was so aesthetically correct, so well arranged—flowers, candles, statues, etc.—and so meticulously clean. Looking for a more intimate place, I walked to the small side chapel, but an older nun was busy blowing out all the candles in front of a large bronze pieta, and made it clear to me that it was time to leave.

It was oddly comforting to leave the well-organized church and return across the rain-drenched field to his temporary home. Not that the circus lacked discipline, but like the community at L'Arche, the circus accepted that life would be messy.

As I walked back to the muddy circus grounds, I wondered how it all fit together. There is no reason to idealize the circus. Much that goes on there is quite unspectacular, inside as well as outside the tent. Nor is there any reason to romanticize the church. Much that goes on there is quite unspiritual. And still, the human heart searches for something larger, something greater than its own pettiness, and everyone who enters the circus or the church is looking for something that reaches out to the stars, or beyond!

Shouldn't there be something of a trapeze artist in every priest and something of a priest in every trapeze artist? I am sure there is, but neither seems to know it!

19

Sunday, May 10 [continued]

The afternoon trapeze act was very poor. There was not much spirit—as if everybody was tired. Karlene missed her layout to Joe. Joe had to let her fall into the net. After that, they finished the routine without much enthusiasm. Afterward Karlene was very depressed. She said: "You want to apologize to everyone and give them their money back. I feel awful."

Tonight I am in a bad mood. Rodleigh became impatient with my questions about the act and started to treat me in a very condescending way, asking me the kind of questions a policeman often asks when he gives you a ticket, such as: "Can't you read the sign that says 50 miles per hour?" I had to remind myself that Rodleigh had had a bad afternoon and that I am a very slow learner.

Tonight is another pull-down night. Forty-five minutes after the show we will be driving into the night to Datteln, the next town, about 57 kilometers away. "Count on an hour and a half," Jennie said. I hate driving in the dark—especially in this camper. But the circus goes on!

Rodleigh and the troupe knew that their trip would be slower with Henri because he drove slowly and cautiously. They consoled themselves that there was an advantage in arriving last to the fair-grounds: if there were problems, the other vehicles would have already discovered them.

Monday, May 11—Datteln

The trip was frightening. Rodleigh led the convoy, using the shortwave radio in his truck to talk with Jon, who, with his big car-avan, drove at the rear. Between Rodleigh's truck and trailer and Jon's caravan were Karlene and Jennie in the Mercedes, which towed Karlene's newly bought house on wheels. Then came Joe with his truck and trailer. I moved in behind Joe and could see Jon behind me in my mirror.

As I said, the trip was scary for me, but not for the others. They are accustomed to driving their mobile homes through the night on the narrow German country roads. But for me it was pure fear! My camper has five gears, and it wasn't easy to figure out which gear to use at different speeds. We kept going slowly at railroad crossings and through sharp bends, and each time I wondered which gear to go back to. It took a long time to get used to it, but eventually I began to feel a little more at ease.

Meanwhile, the fast-driving German cars kept moving in and out of our convoy. They obviously felt we were going too slowly and tried to pass us quickly, but the busy traffic coming toward us made their attempts look like Russian Roulette. Sitting high above the road, I could see this cat-and-mouse game between approaching and pass-ing cars, and I am surprised, still, that nobody was killed.

During trips like this there is ample opportunity to wonder why people are constantly risking their lives. It seems that everyone is so urgently trying to get somewhere that staying alive is less important than getting there!

Rodleigh surveyed the Datteln fairgrounds. They were so water-logged that other artists' trucks were stuck in the mud and would require a tractor to tow them out. Seeing that, he waved the Flying Rodleighs vehicles toward firmer ground, and they parked without problems. Weary from the drive, Henri was almost inarticulate with gratitude when Rodleigh again offered to park his camper van.

Last night, after we had arrived in Datteln, Karlene invited me for a hot drink. I was glad she did. As we spoke it became clear that she was aware of Rodleigh's impatience with me and wanted to make me feel better. "When you have grown up with acrobatics your whole life, you are not always aware that you use a language that is hard for outsiders to understand," she said. Jennie must have talked to her in the car about my conversation with Rodleigh. I was grateful for her kindness and for giving me a renewed sense of belonging.

In his diary the next morning, he continued to muse on the meaning of their traveling show:

As we drove through the night over the curving two-lane roads, crossing one little town after another, I found myself musing about the life of my five trapeze friends. As they move from place to place, they scarcely have time to notice where they are. The circus is usually at the outskirts of town, and the Rodleighs are too busy setting up their rigging, keeping their vehicles in shape, cleaning their trailers, and doing their act to have much time for relaxation.

The many two-day stands are truly exhausting. They arrive in a new town at about midnight and have to spend all the next morning setting up the trapeze. That alone is a four-hour job. Then at 3:30 and 7:00 there are the performances. Although the trapeze act lasts only ten minutes, getting dressed, the preparatory stretching, the evaluation afterwards, the changing of costumes for the finale, and the finale itself keep them quite busy throughout most of the time when the circus is on. During the second morning there is a little time for shopping, making phone calls, and doing business, but the rest of the day is filled again with the trapeze act. Then at 9:00 there is the pull-down and at 10:00 the convoy moves out for the next town.

Last night, as I drove my camper, in a bend in the road I could see the whole convoy in one glance. I thought: "What is this all about? Five people, four huge mobile homes, moving from one little German town to the next, sometimes in rain, sometimes in very cold weather, with never an excuse to stop for a while, to not perform, to not feel up for it, and all that for a ten-minute act that most people forget after they have seen it!"

It's the entertainer's life! Making people say "Ooh" and "Aaaah" and "Wow" and "Nooo"; making them feel tension and release, making them look up to the dome of the tent and say, "How can they do it? I can't believe it," and sending them home with that strange, but quickly passing sensation of having been in another world.

Is my own life very different? I travel here and there giving talks, make people feel safe or excited, and help them come to terms with *their feelings of loss, failure, and anguish, as well as their feelings of growth, success, and joy.*

Am I like circus people—an entertainer? Do I try to hold people up in between the many fragmented moments of their lives and give them a glimpse of "the beyond"? It fascinates me that the word "entertainment" comes from the Latin words inter (between) and tenere (to hold).

What's wrong with being an entertainer? Isn't Jesus the greatest of all entertainers? Isn't He holding people up in a life that constantly wants to go flat? Didn't Jesus come from another world and travel from place to place to let people look up for a moment and realize that there is more to life than they might have thought? And weren't most of those who listened to Jesus like circus-goers, going home with some excitement, but forgetting about it when everyday life reasserted its demands? There were many, many crowds during the three years He went from town to town to announce the Good News, but there were very few for whom His "performance" made a significant difference.

·••••

"THE FIRE TRUCKS ARE here," Dennie announces. "The team will run up the stairs with the stretcher and be here in just a minute to help get you down to the ambulance."

Entertainment is to hold between, "inter-tenere," Henri reminds himself. He knows that he will be well held between the window and the ambulance, but it doesn't strike him as exactly entertaining. Will it be a frightening trip down? He is glad that at least he does not have to drive the truck.

FLYING, FALLING, CATCHING

Monday, May 11 [continued]

This morning I celebrated the Eucharist by myself in the camper. This was the third time during my stay in the circus. I have thought about inviting someone to be with me, but realize that it is better to remain "hidden." The idea of being a priest for the people in this circus has intrigued me, but the longer I am here the more I become convinced that only after a long hidden life here could any type of ministry emerge. The most religious people in this circus seem to be the Muslims from Morocco. I hear them sing at times and it sounds as though they are praying.

Of any Christian form of prayer or worship, however, I see no sign. But Rodleigh's kindness, hospitality, support, and generosity are such a gift to me that it is obvious that I have much more to receive than to give at this time. Right now it appears that I should live here a long time, get to know everybody in a simple and undemanding way, and then it would gradually become clear what ministry would mean.

Wednesday, May 13—Kamen

The trip on the German roads from Datteln to Kamen last night was short but again very tricky for me. At one point I realized I had forgotten to push back my camper's doorstep. Since I was afraid that this piece of metal sticking out was a hazard, I had to stop, walk around the camper, and push it in. Jon, driving behind me, and seeing what was happening, talked by radio to Rodleigh at the front of the convoy, and brought the whole circus troupe to a standstill. At first I couldn't get my camper to start again, but finally I got back on

the road, and everyone started to move again. I felt embarrassed by
my clumsiness, but realized that I had to accept it with a smile.

IT WAS TIME FOR lunch. Jennie glanced at Rodleigh and rolled her eyes.
He knew what she was thinking. Henri had again charged into their
trailer without noticing the mud he tracked in. They had discussed this
with Henri, but he could not remember circus etiquette of removing
his shoes before entering a caravan. He rarely even remembered to
wipe them on the mat. He didn't mean to be rude: he was just oblivious. So Rodleigh and Jennie had privately agreed to overlook it, and
laid down a trail of small rugs at the door and newspapers inside.

Jennie turned away to hide her smile as Henri managed to miss the
newspapers and stomp his muddy shoes onto their carpets again. His
face shone with excitement, eager to discuss how the sodden grounds
were affecting the rigging and stakes of the safety net.

Wednesday, May 13—Kamen [continued]

   Mud, mud, mud. Mud was everywhere at the Kamen fair-
grounds. I walked over to Karlene's place, and we had some coffee.
She was very open with me and spoke about all the "mood swings"
of the troupe. "Rodleigh can be so critical of me. Sometimes I get so
fed up with all his remarks about the way I keep my trailer, the way
I am with my daughter, the way I do my act. A few weeks ago I was
about ready to quit . . . but I have to confess . . . what makes him
so critical is also what makes him such a good artist. He is a real
perfectionist. You have to be a perfectionist when you want to be a
good aerial acrobat. You not only have to do good tricks, but you
have to do them with perfect style. A difficult trick, sloppily executed,

does not make a good show. Well, his perfectionism comes through in all things. I guess I have to learn not to take his criticisms too personally."

Karlene also spoke about Jennie, Joe, and Jon. She spoke of them with great love and respect, but also letting me know that living so closely together, day in day out, with no outside friends, is far from easy. "You really have to give each other space. I need my own space, and I can't deal with people just walking in and out of my trailer all the time."

•••••

SEVERAL FIREFIGHTERS IN BULKY dark uniforms enter Henri's hotel room with a stretcher, a sheet, and a blanket. Dennie moves quickly to unfold the large blanket. He and the firefighters spread it over the stretcher, then cover it with the sheet.

Dennie is speaking to Henri again. "Now everything will come together. We're on our way."

Strong hands smoothly lift Henri, and he is reminded of the Flying Rodleighs lifting him into their arms for a photo. Now Rodleigh pulls up the sides of the blanket to wrap Henri, and brings straps around to buckle him securely in the safety belt—or is it Dennie? Henri's mind is feeling fuzzy: the present moment and the past keep sliding together.

IV

Trust the Catcher

20

Waiting to begin his journey down the narrow hotel hallway, Henri shifts his attention to his own body, noticing the ache in his chest, and that familiar flutter in his gut. Fear? Or maybe not entirely fear. Apprehension—with a hint of curiosity? Even anticipation, despite being in the midst of a medical emergency? His mind wanders again, back to the physical effort and excitement of traveling with the Flying Rodleighs in 1992.

•••••

EVERY DAY HE FELT more and more like a writer, compiling notes for a new kind of writing. His attention in his diary shifted to focus on what kind of book he wanted to write and how to write it.

> *Wednesday, May 13—Kamen [continued]*
> *The longer I am here, the more I find to write about. The flying trapeze act alone could keep me writing for months. I have collected some good personal stories of the three flyers and the two catchers; I*

have a rather good description from Rodleigh of the act itself, but the gaps in my knowledge seem wider than ever.

I know nothing about the rigging. It would take me weeks to figure out the names of its different parts and the way they are pieced together. I know nothing about costumes, the way they are chosen and used. I know nothing about earnings and expenses and the countless administrative aspects of the act.

The more I learn, the more I realize how very little I know. Still, the more details I grasp, the better. I might not use all these details in my final story, but without knowing them I don't think I can make good choices in my writing. This makes me think of Rodin's statue of Balzac in Paris. Although the statue shows Balzac in a wide mantle, the preliminary studies show many nude models. Rodin wanted to know every detail of Balzac's body in order to be able to sculpt him well with the large mantle over his shoulders. I guess this is also true when you want to write a story about the flying trapeze. Even though you don't want to distract your reader with all the technical details, you have to know them quite well if you really want to describe the artistic power of the show.

Thursday, May 14

Reading Jon Franklin's Writing for Story *and Theodore A. Rees Cheney's* Writing Creative Nonfiction *convinces me more and more of the power of writing. I have never really studied the craft of writing, but these books show me how much I have missed.*

As I read these books, surrounded by the circus, I ask myself: "Why are you here? To learn about the circus or to learn how to write?" I now see how they are connected. I love the circus, but I love it so much because it gives me so much to write about. I love to write, but I love it so much because I have the circus to write about. As I read these books on writing, I see how much there is to write about. At first it seemed that the spectacular trapeze act was the main subject, but as I enter more deeply into the circus world while reading these books, I see little stories everywhere and can be away from my camper scarcely more than ten minutes without wanting to run back and report what I have just heard or seen.

So my life here is a strange running to and from the little writing desk in my camper: a strange tension between action and contemplation, between observing and reporting, between listening and writing, between walking around and sitting down.

My main discipline seems to be to remain focused. There is so much to see and hear that I easily get swamped by the countless impressions that come at me from all sides. Constantly I have to remind myself that I cannot go everywhere, cannot speak to everyone, cannot be part of everything.

The Rodleighs give me a good focus. Whatever I can learn from them, I really want to take in. But the rest—the clowns, the magic boys, the animal trainers, the Moroccan workers, and the Polish musicians—must remain on the periphery of my vision. Otherwise everything starts spinning, and writing becomes impossible.

Henri turned back to his *Writing Creative Nonfiction* book and read, "Faced with the search for structure, sit back and sift, shuffle and stack. Do any patterns, or things that look like possible patterns, take shape? . . . If the ending is there, it'll act as a magnetic pole drawing everything toward it." He marked the paragraph to make it easier to find later. Returning to his diary he noted:

Thursday, May 14 [continued]

I am convinced that I have been sent to the Rodleighs to discover something new about life and death, love and fear, peace and conflict, Heaven and Hell, something I can't get to know and write about in any other way.

Often I think: "How could I have ever imagined, even a few years ago, that I would sit for a few weeks writing in a camper in the midst of a circus in Germany?" But here I am, and it feels like the only good place to be right now. What tomorrow will bring, I will find out tomorrow. I am happy that I don't have to know that today.

During the afternoon show, just after Karlene had explained to me about the socks filled with magnesium-carbonate powder to dry the hands of the flyers and catchers, Joe's sock came loose and fell from the catch bar into the net. Rodleigh pointed to it, but nothing could be done, since the act was in full swing. The Moroccan ringman smiled at me when he noticed that I had seen it happen.

The act went on as usual, but during the evaluation Karlene told me that it had scared her. "Joe sweats a lot, and he needs it to keep his hands dry in order to hold on to us."

The evening show went badly for Rodleigh. He missed the full-twist somersault and on his return he hit his calves at the pedestal board. After the act he was limping badly, but Jennie didn't make a big drama of it. "It is a strange place to get hurt," she said. "That has never happened before."

Friday, May 15—Wuppertal

We made it all right to the fairgrounds in the center of Wuppertal, despite my missing the exit to the freeway and Jon's having to go after me and bring me back to the convoy, and even despite Rodleigh's

turning off the freeway too early and having the whole convoy wan-
dering back and forth at the wrong end of town. When, by midnight,
all our trailers were neatly lined up, we felt some real excitement
about our new location. "I saw a large supermarket just before we
entered the grounds," said Karlene. Joe exclaimed: "Finally, a place
we can stay a while." Jennie remarked: "Except for not having grass,
we call this an ideal place," and Rodleigh added: "Nice and close
to the tent so we can hear the music and know when our time in
the show is coming." Jon was in an especially good mood because
his parents were arriving the following day from Detroit for a week.

This morning I decided to take the afternoon train to Freiburg to
visit friends. I felt a certain sadness about leaving, but was glad to
know that I would be back within a week and still be able to spend a
few days with the circus in Wuppertal.

Rodleigh stayed to do the rigging while Jennie took Henri to the
railway station. But first they checked Henri's caravan to make sure
that his electrical and gas appliances were turned off. After ten days
of traveling together, they were getting the hang of living with Henri.

21

In Freiburg, Henri eagerly laid out his thoughts about the trapeze to his friend and editor Franz Johna. After all, Franz had been with him that first night at the circus with his father.

Sunday, May 17—Freiburg

I sense that Franz still has some problems with my enthusiasm for the circus. In his presence, I feel as though I should choose a more serious subject. He finds it hard to see how this could lead to a spiritual book. But as we spoke, and as I explained that I wasn't thinking of using the Rodleighs as illustrations for great spiritual truths, but was simply trying to write a good story about good people who are doing good things, Franz began to warm up and even got excited.

It is important for me to be away from the circus and to be invited to "defend" my project. The more I talk about it, the more I realize that, first of all, I want to write a good story and that I have to trust that the story, alone, will carry within itself Good News.

Henri meandered along the side streets of downtown Freiburg, thinking happily, *Freiburg has become for me like a second hometown.* He bought a few new Vincent van Gogh prints. He didn't miss teaching university, but he enjoyed observing the many students with their briefcases going to and coming from various handsome old university buildings. *Just being here!* he exulted to himself.

Monday, May 18

I spent a good hour with Franz. We spoke mostly about writing a book with meditations for every day. Franz had already published such a book with daily readings by Carlo Martini, Carlo Caretto, and Heinrich Spaemann—compilations of excerpts from their earlier writings.

I wasn't too excited about doing another anthology. Many of my books no longer express my spiritual vision and, although I am not dismissing my earlier writing as no longer valid, I feel that something radically different is being asked of me.

My many encounters with people who have no contact with any church, my contact with AIDS patients, my experience in the circus, and the many socio-political events of the past few years all ask for a new way to speak about God. This new way includes not only content but form. Not only what I say, but also how I say it should be different.

What mostly comes to mind is stories. I know I have to write stories. Not essays with arguments, quotes, and analyses, but stories which are short and simple and give us a glimpse of God in the midst of our multifaceted lives.

The next day Henri spent the whole day at his desk, writing. The apartment on the third floor of Franz and Reny Johna's house was familiar and comfortable, and had always been a good place for him to write.

But I feel a certain inner resistance to working on the circus book, as if the project is too big for me and I still do not have enough knowledge about the trapeze to write it easily. Perhaps, he thought, he still was too much an observer. *I am still not fully capable of writing from within.* He tried to encourage himself that there was no end to the process of becoming part of one's subject, so just start writing, trusting that something will emerge. As he gradually slowed down, writing became easier.

But his visit was soon over.

Thursday, May 21—Wuppertal

This morning Franz took me to the railroad station. At 1:30 I was back at the circus. I had been wondering on the train how the week had been going for the Flying Rodleighs. Was Rodleigh's leg healed? Had there been a good audience during this long stay in one place? Would I find everyone in good spirits, less tired and frazzled than when I had left?

I soon discovered that it hadn't been an easy week at all. Rodleigh's injury still looked bad. Karlene had some internal bleeding in her stomach area, spent hours at the doctor's office, and was finally told that it was impossible to do any trapeze work as long as there was pain. Jennie had an extended medical checkup because of her heart murmur. The German clown collapsed in the ring as a result of a dust allergy and was taken to the hospital. Mrs. Kaminski fell from the Russian bar when she came down from her final trick; she hurt her leg badly. Peter, the Englishman with his dog act, had a real setback:

the clown's dog got loose and went after Peter's little circus dog and bit him so badly that Peter had to keep him out of the ring for nearly a week. And all the Hassani tumbling boys seem to have pain in their wrists and ankles!

Somewhat apprehensive, I went to the afternoon show, wondering how the trapeze act would go with two wounded artists. At first, nothing seemed too different. But when Rodleigh worked with Jon and wanted to make a front somersault from Jon to Joe, he failed to reach Joe's hands and came down into the net. Since he had planned to return from Joe to Jon and do some more tricks from Jon's hands, his fall forced him to cut all of that out and let Jennie continue the act from the pedestal board.

But the evening performance was completely different. Was it the simple determination to work well together in hard circumstances? Was it the large and enthusiastic audience? I don't know, and the Rodleighs probably didn't know, either, but the show was superb. Rodleigh flew to and from Jon and Joe with great ease and was caught without any visible strain. He made his somersaults and twists with tremendous grace and moved through the air as if the air was his. Jennie too went from the board and returned to it with much elegance, and when Jennie and Rodleigh concluded the act with their spectacular passage over the flying bar from and into the hands of Joe, the audience exploded in a burst of applause and foot stomping that made Gerd Simoneit send the whole troupe back into the ring for another bow.

The whole group was excited; they had felt the electricity in the air. Even Joe, who is usually quite reserved, didn't hide his enthusiasm. "It went really well," he said.

The next day, Henri deliberately spent the intermission with Jon's sister, who was visiting. He had been struck by an instruction in Cheney's *Writing Creative Nonfiction*, because it was something that came easily to him: "Listen to everyone—unsolicited comments by 'unimportant people' may explain even more than those received from the 'notables.'"

Saturday, May 23—Geysteren

Last night, during the intermission, I didn't join the Rodleighs for their evaluation, but spoke instead with Jon's sister Kristen, who has been going to every show since she arrived here with her parents from Detroit. Kristen loves the circus and can't get enough of it.

For a woman with Down's syndrome, she is very independent and quite articulate. The clowns, with their "boxing act" full of heavy sounding blows, were her favorites. She told me all about her family, her work, and her role in the Special Olympics, where she won two medals and a ribbon.

As we spoke I realized that the circus speaks not only to the young as well as to the old, but also to mentally handicapped people as well as to the sophisticated. Indeed, the circus has found a universal language that bridges many differences among people.

On this, my last day in the circus, I saw many connections between my L'Arche community in Toronto and this circus community. From a distance they seem so different, but looking at them closely they are quite similar. They are both communities for special people.

Saying good-bye wasn't easy after so many good days with such good people. But I felt ready to move on. I know the Rodleighs will be my friends for life. They might not yet know this, but leaving them last night didn't seem to be a leaving for very long. Just a time to gather up all my new impressions and find the story that lies beneath them.

After affectionate farewells in the early morning, Henri climbed behind the wheel and drove his camper van away from the circus in his characteristic way. Rodleigh winced as he watched Henri come very close to a parked car as he drove over a curb.

At 6 o'clock this morning, I left the fairgrounds in Wuppertal. An hour and a half later I crossed the border into the Netherlands and at 8:30 I was home with my father in Geysteren. He was very happy to see me and wanted to know all about the circus.

22

At the hotel in Hilversum, the ambulance driver shoves a large red emergency bag into Dennie's hands. Dennie pulls out some extra medication.

"I will keep this with us in case we need it in the next few minutes," he tells Henri. One of the firefighters is already waiting by the door with Henri's carry-on bag. Dennie hands the emergency bag back to the driver, who runs out the door with the firefighter. "They are heading downstairs to meet us at the bottom," Dennie adds.

He pauses, concerned by Henri's lack of response. Is he distracted by pain, is he afraid, or is he losing consciousness? Dennie keeps talking to keep Henri alert and present: "Now we are ready to go down the hall to the window. The hotel has opened it for us, and we will load your stretcher onto the aerial lift. Don't worry. I will be with you all the way."

The blanket wrapped around Henri is warm. Henri opens his eyes and tries to smile at Dennie, but realizes Dennie cannot see his mouth twitch behind the oxygen mask. Dennie tucks the oxygen bottle securely between Henri's legs. The heart monitor is held by one of the firefighters, who stays close so that the three leads remain firmly attached to Henri's chest. Another is preparing to carry the IV bag. He is impressed by their care and coordination as they confidently reach for the equipment they need. Each seems to know immediately what is needed and take their role without confusion. They must practice this.

It's another version of reaching out, Henri thinks. *Reaching Out* was the title of his second book, and Henri finds himself pondering how that book's main points are like the trapeze. From the pedestal, the flyer has to reach out to the trapeze bar. The catcher reaches out for the flyer. Even the book's subtitle emphasized motion and momentum: *The Three Movements of the Spiritual Life.* When he wrote the book twenty-one years ago, he articulated an *inward movement* from loneliness to solitude, then an *outward journey* from hostility to hospitality, and finally an *upward movement* from illusion to prayer. Readers found it practical and helpful, a spiritual self-help book just as the genre was starting to take hold, and it became Henri's first "best-seller."

But now, blearily watching Dennie and the careful teamwork of his rescuers, Henri wonders if he was thinking too much of a spirituality for just the individual. How could anyone reach out in those ways alone? Without a sense of being part of a larger body, even a team or community? The question isn't new. Already in 1983 while he was living in Latin America, Henri's new friends revealed to him *how individualistic and elitist my own spirituality had been. It was hard to confess, but true, that in many respects my thinking about the spiritual life had been deeply influenced by my North American milieu with its emphasis upon the "interior life" and the methods and techniques for developing that life.*

In fact, Henri reflected, he had fallen into *a spirituality for intro-*

spective persons who have the luxury of the time and space needed to develop inner harmony and quietude. Very different from the attentive, urgent, disciplined focus of Dennie's colleagues. Or of the Flying Rodleighs.

What do I want to say about the teamwork of the trapeze act? Henri asks himself now. Is beauty in its essence a shared spiritual endeavor? These artists have a desire for continual self-improvement, but they create beauty for others, and their act is lived out in teamwork and community. *I've seen very clearly that all together form one body, as a whole. If one part of the body isn't functioning, the whole body isn't functioning.*

. . . . •

BY THE END OF his time traveling with the Rodleighs in 1992, Henri felt excited about his project and eager to continue to learn how to write differently. Less than two weeks after Henri lurched away in his camper van, Rodleigh received a letter, thanking them for their kindness and hospitality. Henri confided that he now had lots of material for his book, and was considering writing it as his first attempt at a book for a secular audience.

Who would understand the wide-ranging connections he was seeing? On June 2, he wrote to John Dear, an American friend committed to community building and peacemaking, *One day I hope to be able to tell you about a very interesting month I spent recently with a German circus. In some ways, life in a circus is not dissimilar to life in a community of nonviolence.*

At the end of November, Henri again wrote to Rodleigh, now announcing that his ideas had swung back to introducing a religious element into the book and staying in more familiar writing territory.

Rodleigh chuckled to himself, privately wondering how Henri would be able to find enough connections between the Flying Rodleighs trapeze act and any religious topic to fill a book.

After sending his letter to Rodleigh, Henri picked up his pen feeling inspired. He could easily imagine using three movements as a way to tell the story of the Rodleighs. That format was both familiar and had been enormously successful. Readers loved it. He was excited as he scribbled out a draft outline of three movements. Each connected the Flying Rodleighs to his L'Arche community and to the Church.

From career to vocation, he wrote. This first movement would include *the personal journeys of each member of the troupe. Many assistants at L'Arche Daybreak had made similar choices.*

The second movement was from *individualism to community.* Henri outlined this section with a rush of enthusiasm. *To realize their vocation, the Flying Rodleighs had to live together because everything in the act depended on their teamwork and their care for each other. There could be no competition among them, no heroes, no anger or jealousy, and they had to practice their act continually together.* In other words, it was like L'Arche: *a lifestyle lived out in community with compassion, forgiveness, and a shared rhythm of life. "Look how they love each other!" is how Jesus said Christians would be recognized, and the same was true of the circus community.* Henri reread his notes, thinking about all the ways this section could help many of the lonely people who wrote letters to him.

Finally, he envisioned a third movement *from entertainment to inspiration.* He had been thinking about this ever since he journaled about entertainment on his road trip with the circus. *The point of the trapeze act is not just to distract people but to give them a glimpse of the beauty of life. Not only artistic beauty, but a beautiful vision of humanity in harmony, where it is possible for people to feel safe with one another.* In fact, the Flying Rodleighs offered *a vision of amazement, joy, rapture, beauty, elegance*—Henri's words tumbled over each other as he wrote. He imagined members of the audience like himself thinking, *I am not simply forgetting my trouble but I see who I am, can be, and want to be.* In that way, *the trapeze act is for others,* he wrote, *because it reveals the life of vocation and community, as does L'Arche.*

Then something shifted. Henri felt his shoulders droop. He put down his pen and hugged his chest tight, looking out the window beside his desk. The book he was outlining looked competent and full of important insights. The sections about the trapeze engaged him, but his energy dwindled and his focus slipped as he tried to outline the accompanying sections about L'Arche. By the time he tried to apply each insight to the spiritual life, he completely lost interest in his own subject.

He sighed as he admitted to himself that he had no real enthusiasm for this way of framing his experience. Perhaps the problem was that *Reaching Out* was published many years earlier. If his book about the Rodleighs also explored three spiritual movements, would he be like those exquisite Russian performers? Having created and perfected one act, the Kaminskis would do only that act for the rest of their careers.

Henri didn't want to have one trick, performing the same feat of writing again and again, even if his audience applauded every time. Like Rodleigh, Henri wanted continually to change his act, take a risk, try something new, even if it might fail or be uncomfortable. He abandoned the outline.

"I don't want to write just another book," he said to an interviewer a year later.

> *A lot of people have said, "Why don't you write another book about prayer, another book about God, another book about meditation?"*
>
> *No, no, I want to write a book about the trapeze.*
>
> *And they say, "What have you got in your head? Are you crazy?"*
>
> *No, I'm not crazy, I'm just in love with the trapeze and with God and the two have something to do with each other.*

Every time Henri returned to his trapeze book, he felt a sense of being called. He had explained this in his earlier diary, while on the road with the circus:

> *Why should I write about a trapeze act? I have no answers. The trapeze act was "given" to me last year, just as the print of Rembrandt's "The Return of the Prodigal Son" was "given" to me in 1983.*
>
> *There is a strange "must" to my writing about the trapeze act. I still do not know precisely why the Flying Rodleighs are so important for me. I still cannot articulate fully the meaning of their show. But I know with great inner certainty that they hold an important secret for me that will reveal itself little by little if I remain faithful to my intuition.*

23

Yes, he thinks, the trapeze was "given" to him. He had felt an immediate mysterious, physical connection. His most similar experience had occurred years earlier.

.....

It was 1983. Sitting in his friend Simone's small room at the L'Arche community in Trosly, France, Henri lost track of their conversation, distracted by her poster of Rembrandt's painting. His attention was utterly sucked into the scene before him. A son in ragged clothing was on his knees, leaning his head against his aged father, who stood tenderly laying both his hands on his son's back. The painting illustrated a story Jesus had told, about a younger son who demanded his inheritance, left home, and wasted it in extravagant, prodigal living. When he ran out of money and friends, the son returned home to his father, ashamed. But instead of rebuking him, the openhearted father embraced him, then hosted a homecoming party. His older brother, who had obediently stayed home, resented that his father took him for granted while welcoming home his irresponsible brother with a big feast. The painting showed not only the tender reunion of the father and younger son, but also the brooding anger of the older son.

The moment Henri saw it, he was immersed, convinced that the Rembrandt image had been "given" to him, bursting into his life as something so profound that he felt it in his own body.

So he meditated on Rembrandt's painting for several years. He carried small copies of it to give away on his travels, used a large poster-sized version for retreats, showed it to everyone, and thought about it endlessly. Yet for several years, he could not find a way to write about that painting that had gripped him so dramatically. A book just wasn't taking shape for him.

When he fell apart in a complete emotional and psychological and spiritual breakdown in 1987, he carried his Rembrandt print with him. From Daybreak to England then to Winnipeg, the days turned into weeks, and he looked at the image each day and through his long nights. It hovered always at the edge of his consciousness, even when he lay curled up on the floor moaning.

Stripped of his sense of self and security, mysteriously Henri started to find himself on the inside of the painting he had contemplated for so long. Slowly insights came. Not all at once, and not in a simple way. His identification with the younger son deepened. Now he felt as helpless, lost, and needy as that son, full of self-rejection and disgust. He tried to love that son. In England, his friend Bart Gavigan urged Henri to see himself also in the older son. Henri was the oldest son in his family, obedient and faithful, yet he had to admit that he often seethed with resentment and self-righteousness. Yearning for freedom, and for love without conditions, he felt envious of the courage and adventures of the younger son, who dared to set out and take a risk, even if it turned out badly.

As he began to find some peace in his own body, in his body's truth, his friend Sue offered a new insight. "Henri, whether you are the younger son or the elder son, you have to realize that you are called to become the father," she said. And suddenly more than five years of immersion in Rembrandt's painting snapped into focus.

These deeper self-reflections offered a way into the painting that anyone could share, finding their own feelings mirrored in the sons and the father. As he recovered his confidence, Henri offered retreats and talks about Rembrandt's painting, trying to articulate his own life through Rembrandt's image so that others could discover their own parallel experiences. The response was tremendous, and Henri felt encouraged each time that he could write with the authority of his own vulnerability. But it took a long time. Even with that depth of insight, another four years went by before the book was published.

When the book was done, he tried a few titles, starting with *A Dreadful Mercy*. Nobody liked that. He tried *A Dreadful Love*, then revised it to *Canvas of Love*. He resisted titling the book after Rembrandt's painting or Jesus's parable, because the word "prodigal" seemed archaic, and he hoped to reach a wider audience. His editors, however, convinced him that his readers would respond well to a book titled after both the painting and the parable.

His book *The Return of the Prodigal Son* was published in 1992, subtitled *A Meditation on Fathers, Brothers and Sons*. He dedicated it to his father, who was turning ninety. But like his books *Letters to Marc,* which he wrote for his nephew and other young readers, and *Life of the Beloved,* composed for a secular Jewish friend and others like him,

Henri's intended audience didn't flock to his book. *The Return of the Prodigal Son* did not catch on with men involved in the 1990s men's movement. Instead, it became enormously popular among clergy and spiritual seekers of all denominations.

For the second printing of his Prodigal Son book, Henri changed the subtitle to *A Story of Homecoming*.

.·····•

WELL, HENRI THINKS NOW, perhaps my trapeze book will reach an audience completely different from the one I imagine. But the real point is that from the time Rembrandt's painting exploded into his life until that book was complete, nine years passed.

Relax, he tells himself. You saw the Flying Rodleighs five years ago. Somewhere inside you, it's all in motion.

It's all about motion, he realizes. Unlike a painting, nothing in a traveling trapeze act stays still. In fact, when he first watched the Rodleighs practice five years earlier, it was the movement and dynamism of the act that captivated him.

> *They were trying to do something new, and it was absolutely fascinating to see because it was very very difficult and they couldn't do it. It was a jump from one platform, they swing, they swing back, and then they make a salto—Rod was doing that and he was caught at the other end by Joe, one of the catchers. And then Joe threw him up, up to the high top where Jon Griggs was hanging and he caught him there in the middle, right in the middle of the circus, and then he had to throw him back to Joe, and then Rod goes with Joe back to the platform again.*

THEIR STRUGGLE TO GET it right struck something deep in Henri—not just the swing of the flyer, but flyer and catchers whirling together, their momentum and energy feeding off each other. The soaring flyer had faith that the catcher would grab them to renew their momentum, then launch them onward to the next catcher. Trust and risk in continued motion together.

24

Henri twitches involuntarily. Now his fragile body is actually participating in physical risk. The sense of risk that he tried to grasp back in 1992 at the workshop with Bart seems comically theoretical and disembodied now that his body will soon be suspended in the air, at the top of the Hilversum fire department's aerial lift.

His chest still hurts, but not alarmingly. Henri is not worried. It will be a warning. He is being cared for, and he is only sixty-four. He even feels oddly relieved that this interruption has happened here in his home country, so that his father and brothers and sister can come to be with him.

Henri feels a surge of excitement as six uniformed firefighters surround him, lifting the stretcher and carrying it down the hall together. This is amazing: I have a disciplined and skilled troupe of rescuers preparing me to fly, marvels Henri.

When I saw the Flying Rodleighs for the first time, I had a feeling that they expressed one of my deepest inner longings to be totally free, as well as totally safe.

He feels very safe.

To me it's very fascinating that this art can only function when all the members give full concentration to each other. They constantly have to be aware of where everyone is. Then there is harmony. The beauty of human communion becomes visible in this act.

·····

HENRI'S FRIEND FRANK HAMILTON read Henri's 1992 journal about driving his caravan with the Flying Rodleighs and it scared him. He knew that Henri was not the most attentive driver. In fact, his driving was notorious. In his journal he wrote about driving through little towns and down dark roads at one o'clock in the morning.

So in 1993, when Frank heard that Henri was again planning a visit with the Flying Rodleighs, he said, "Henri, you're going to Germany next June. May I go with you?"

Henri pondered this. The Rodleighs had started to feel like family. Would it work to add a friend to his visit?

"Why?" asked Henri.

"Because I could maybe help you with the driving," offered Frank. Frank was a steady long-term friend, a chaplain in the US military.

It didn't take long for Henri to decide, "You know, I would like that! I could relax with you driving and it would be fun to go together. I feel secure with you."

Henri began to imagine a new version of his trapeze project: a novel, beautifully illustrated with photos. Photographer Ron P. van den Bosch had known Henri for more than twenty-five years and they had collaborated on several books, but he was still startled when Henri broached the possibility of a new project together at the reception after a family funeral in Holland. After taking off his priestly robes but even before he had a coffee or a sandwich, Henri urgently asked Ron if he had any plans at the beginning of June, a few weeks later. When Ron said he was free, Henri explained that he wanted Ron to join him in Germany to take pictures of trapeze artists in a traveling circus. Struck by how swiftly Henri's attention was moving on from the sorrow of the funeral, Ron sipped his coffee and took his time answering. He was reminded of films about gangsters who make agreements and close deals at their many funerals. But Henri's bright eyes and eager enthusiasm were irresistible.

I came to know the trapeze life from within. I came to know how Rodleigh, and his wife, and his sister, and his friends were relating to each other. I came to know the danger of what they were doing. I came to know how complicated everything is around this one act— setting up the rigging, preparing, the costumes, the sound, the music. This one little act was a whole life, and what happens in these ten minutes was really the result of a life of work, a life of thinking, a life of commitment, a life of enthusiasm, and this really absolutely fascinated me. I just wanted to grab it from the inside.

The Flying Rodleighs eagerly agreed when Henri proposed another visit. They also were not surprised that Henri chose a time when they had an extended booking in one place so that he could stay at a local hotel rather than drive a caravan on the road with them.

Henri arrived with Frank in June 1993. Rodleigh and the whole troupe greeted Henri as a member of the family, pleased to see Henri bursting with his usual enthusiasm. Rodleigh felt a bit at a disadvantage, however, when Frank knew much more about the Flying Rodleighs than they knew about him. Soon Ron arrived and also greeted the entire troupe as though they were old friends. Clearly Henri liked talking about them.

Henri presented his plan: Ron would take a collection of high-quality photos for Henri's book. As Ron snapped pictures of the troupe setting up the rigging, Rodleigh noted that Ron seemed blissfully unaware that the troupe might find it hard to behave naturally with a camera lens right in their faces. Even Henri's friends were charmingly oblivious to their impact on others.

Henri was buzzing with pride. To Rodleigh, he seemed even more moved watching their act again, now that he had someone to share it with. Henri brought Frank and Ron for the traditional tea and biscuits after the show, and Henri and the Rodleighs caught up on their last few months. Henri was glad that Karlene's torn stomach muscle had healed well and she was again performing. Rodleigh showed Henri a video taken in Rome that showed his triple somersault, something he was not able to do with Circus Barum because the tent was not large enough. Henri loved the beauty of the move and watched it several times in slow motion.

When Henri, Frank, and Ron left, it was late and quiet on the circus grounds and Rodleigh could hear them talking excitedly almost all the way back to their hotel.

"What do you think?" Henri asked his friends earnestly as they walked through the quiet fairgrounds. "I don't know why I can't get started on this book. What do you think is the secret of my attraction to the Flying Rodleighs?"

Frank and Ron burst out laughing. "Well maybe, just maybe, because they are stunningly beautiful people, Henri!" chortled Frank. Ron added, "Did you happen to notice that they all have wonderful physiques as well as beautiful form?"

Henri pondered this for a moment. "I guess like Cirque du Soleil, they offer a very sensual circus experience. But I love the Flying Rodleighs performance much more."

"Sure," said Frank. "That makes sense. You admire their human bodies and acrobatic act, but you also have become close enough to touch them in their minds and even perhaps their souls. It puts the flesh and blood on them, so for you they are real people, not just a fantasy."

"Their artistry is beautiful," Ron reflected, "especially how they interact."

"Yes! And it's even more than that!" Henri enthused. "It's the way they have invited me into their lives. You know, they aren't religious people, but I think they have a spiritual hunger that they don't know how to talk about. And when I see them fly, I am in touch with a hunger in me that I don't know how to talk about, either."

Jennie's lunch the next day received lavish praise from Frank and Ron, while Henri was so caught up in explaining the lives of the performers that he barely noticed what he was eating. In the days that followed, they attended all the shows, enjoyed visits with each member of the troupe, and took many rolls of film.

One afternoon, Henri urged Ron to take a photo of himself and Frank with the troupe. Without Henri noticing, Rodleigh motioned to the others to pick Henri up in their arms and support him horizontally.

"Look at him, content as a Roman emperor being fed grapes by his servants," Rodleigh joked. "If he were a cat, he would purr!"

Ironically, the photos did not turn out, and Henri eagerly requested a repeat posing the next day, as relaxed and delighted as on the first spontaneous lift.

25

The highlight of the 1993 visit was on June 6, when Henri accepted Rodleigh's invitation to swing on the trapeze. Henri noted with some trepidation that the rungs of the rope ladder to the platform seemed uneven, with different spaces at different heights, but he hesitated for only a moment, then boldly started to climb as a helper held the ladder to minimize its swing. His eyes wide with concentration, Henri carefully climbed in his stiff leather-soled shoes and dress trousers. At the top, Karlene helped him onto the pedestal, and from that high vantage point they watched Rodleigh practice a double layout from Jon to Joe, testing out the height. He has to be high enough for Joe to catch him, explained Karlene.

I hold on to the pedestal with more fear than necessary. It is a safe place but I still feel somewhat anxious when I look down into the net and see the Sunday morning visitors on the seats. After his practice with Jon, Rodleigh comes up to the pedestal with the safety belt. Karlene puts the safety belt around me and Rodleigh hooks me on to the ropes. He powders my hands and asks me to hold onto the bar. It feels like taking a risk because the bar is a good distance from the pedestal. Rodleigh says: "Don't be afraid. I will hold you and drop you off the pedestal when you have a good grip with both hands on the bar."

He gives the instruction: "Keep your legs straight as you swing. Don't bend your knees. When you are ready to fall in the net, wait until I say 'hop' and then let your hands go, lift up your legs, so you fall into the net in a sitting position."

I grab on to the bar with one hand. Rodleigh stands behind me and embraces me around my waist. Then I put my other hand on the bar: "Keep your arms straight," Rodleigh says. Then he lifts me off the pedestal.

It feels great to swing through the circus tent. It is not scary. Just swinging back and forth. Ron stands on the King pole balcony and takes some pictures. After a few swings Rodleigh calls: "Next swing— let go." Then he calls: "Hop." I let go of the bar, lift my front feet, and fall in the net. The net is not as far away as I thought. Joe, who holds the ropes connected with the safety belt, makes the fall even lighter. I lie on my back in the net. People in the "audience" clap, laughing.

Rodleigh enjoyed seeing Henri on the platform, looking ready to explode with delight. Rodleigh was also interested in Henri's confidence. Most beginners show fear, but Henri seemed to have no fear of the height. He just wanted to reach out and grab the trapeze bar and swing. Rodleigh explained carefully to Henri what he needed to do, especially how to listen to Rodleigh's commands to ensure his safe landing in the net. Henri nodded earnestly in confirmation, but looking back Rodleigh realized that the silly grin on Henri's face should have alerted him that Henri was not actually absorbing anything Rodleigh said. The safety belt turned out to be a good decision.

Henri's eyes grew a few sizes larger as he left the pedestal board. Rodleigh wondered if Henri's involuntary gasp expressed fear or a quick call to his guardian angel, whom Rodleigh figured must be kept busy constantly looking after Henri. Henri's reaction to Rodleigh's call to let go and land in the net was hopelessly late and instead of landing in a sitting position, he put his feet down first. Joe supported his weight by holding firmly to the rope that was attached to the safety belt, then gradually loosened the rope to allow gravity to complete Henri's far-from-graceful landing in the net. Henri had no idea that he had not performed his fall perfectly. Rodleigh said Henri was smiling so hard that if it weren't for his ears, his lips would have touched behind his head!

Henri stood up gingerly in the net and tried to walk. The net bounced. His feet moved faster than his body. When it looked like he might catapult right off the net, Joe pulled on the ropes holding his belt to slow him down. Henri tried to turn, but the belt ropes twisted so he had to turn the other way, and then as the ropes pulled him, Henri began to negotiate the almost forty-foot trip backward, increasing in speed involuntarily, much to the mirth of his audience. Their laughing reached a crescendo when Joe mischievously loosened his grip on the ropes that Henri was using to help balance, and he landed unceremoniously on his back with his skinny legs waving above him. Even he saw the comedy. The whole atmosphere was lighthearted, the kind of scene that remains imprinted in the memory. Rodleigh treasured it: the laughter and friendship, Henri right in the middle with that everlasting smile on his face as he lay in the net after his great swing on the trapeze.

Rodleigh invites me to give it a second try. Again I climb up to the pedestal, get lifted off by Rodleigh, swing and fall in the net. Only afterwards I realize that I didn't use the opportunity to push the swing higher up and make some larger strokes. I did feel tired quickly and realized that my nervousness combined with my untrained muscle made me unable to try it a third time.

When Henri, Ron, and Frank returned to their hotel, they began brainstorming about Henri's book. "I really like them, Henri," began Frank. "I think they are hungry to sit down with someone like you, and not because they are impressed by your credentials."

Henri agreed. "They are wonderful, searching, beautiful people. But it is so good for me, too. I feel grounded by knowing them, maybe a bit like I feel around Adam at Daybreak. And they affirm me in a new way. I can give something different to them."

He pulled out his simple black hardcover notebook and settled into an armchair to jot down notes. "What do you think? What should I say in my book?" he asked.

"The act is like a Russian icon, which by distorting the natural world invites a viewer into a spiritual world," offered Frank.

They began to frame the trapeze act in mythic terms. The men—Rodleigh, Jon, and Joe—were *handsome, graceful, well formed, photogenic and strong, catching fair damsels and one another as they flew through the air.* They also *rescued one another from danger, falls, and death.*

But members of the troupe were not only mythic but unique individuals. If Henri were to write in a more creative way, he would need to bring each character vividly to life using specific details. Henri continued to write notes, now with the new subheading *Real People.* He began with Jennie: *Makes their caravan a warm, clean, and comfort-*

able home. *Never idle—designing and hand-sewing complex patterns for their sequined costumes.*

Rodleigh, they decided, represented *Integrity and Wholeness.* His sister Karlene was identified as a *Survivor* of some bad experiences, now carrying multiple roles as parent and provider to Kail.

Frank commented on the *Hospitality, Kindness, Attentiveness* of the troupe. They continued with notes on *Physique: Rod, Jon + Joe—Handsome, well built—Strong beautiful + intense faces.*

They were having fun. Frank conjured up menu items to describe the American Jon: *crew cut hair, with a wholesome buttermilk + cornbread sense about himself. A bit of a ham—loves to be photographed.* Regarding Joe, Frank commented, *I want to say, "Joe—you are neat."* The three friends nodded. There was something about Joe that touched them. *Dark wavy hair, deep dimples, turquoise earring, stutters. Short, fat hands + arms—muscular + graceful,* wrote Henri.

"But how can I communicate the profoundly embodied spiritual quality of the experience?" Henri asked. They considered this together. Soon Henri, Frank, and Ron were getting quite elated finding ways to express the intensely physical performance.

Ron commented, *"It's like people making love! Think about it: Bodies in tandem with one another, Harmony, Precision. They interact in the Air as lovers who have a good time."*

"Yup," added Frank. *"It's lovemaking season in heaven!"*

"And then afterward, all the participants have a discussion of the flaws," chortled Henri.

They nearly fell off their chairs laughing. Henri, speedily writing all this down, couldn't quite imagine how to write a book that would catch that kind of shared mirth, but he wished he could.

26

Rodleigh did not see Henri again until a brief visit in November 1993 when Henri returned with Ron and his daughter Marieke. Securely anchored in a safety belt, Henri amused everyone with his unique moves on the trampoline. He speedily ate the hearty lunch provided by Jennie and worried that Rodleigh was taking too many risks in developing a new act. Even knowing that the life of traveling circus performers was one of constant changes requiring attention and flexibility, he was concerned about how the new troupe member Slava fit into the act and whether that had implications for his research and book. After spending the night on the sofa in Jon's trailer, he left the next morning—a short visit with another fond farewell, reflected Rodleigh.

When Henri sent him a copy of *Our Greatest Gift* the next spring, Rodleigh hoped Henri would never know that he had not read any of the other books Henri had given him. It was not that he had no religious background, actually the reverse. He and Karlene had been raised as Seventh-day Adventists, a church that disapproved of what it considered the decadent, countercultural circus life. Rodleigh's call to be a circus performer was so compelling, however, that he followed it even though it meant leaving his faith community. Ever since then he was wary of judgmental religious beliefs that could pull him into self-doubt and guilt.

But Henri was different. Rodleigh was curious to see what Henri would write about his perspective on the Flying Rodleighs themselves. He looked at the slim hardcover book with its attractive cream-colored cover, read the friendly inscription from Henri, then flipped to the pages Henri identified in the accompanying letter.

> One day, I was sitting with Rodleigh, the leader of the troupe, in his caravan, talking about flying. He said, "As a flyer, I must have complete trust in my catcher. The public might think that I am the great star of the trapeze, but the real star is Joe, my catcher. He has to be there for me with split-second precision and grab me out of the air as I come to him in the long jump."
>
> "How does it work?" I asked.
>
> "The secret," Rodleigh said, "is that the flyer does nothing and the catcher does everything. When I fly to Joe, I have simply to stretch out my arms and hands and wait for him to catch me and pull me safely over the apron behind the catch bar."
>
> "You do nothing!" I said, surprised.
>
> "Nothing," Rodleigh repeated. "The worst thing the flyer can do is to try to catch the catcher. I am not supposed to catch Joe. It's Joe's task to catch me. If I grabbed Joe's wrists, I might break them, or he might break mine, and that would be the end for both of us. A flyer must fly, and a catcher must catch, and the flyer must trust, with outstretched arms, that his catcher will be there for him."
>
> When Rodleigh said this with so much conviction, the words of

Jesus flashed through my mind: "Father into your hands I commend my Spirit." Dying is trusting in the catcher. To care for the dying is to say, "Don't be afraid. Remember that you are the beloved child of God. He will be there when you make your long jump. Don't try to grab him; he will grab you. Just stretch out your arms and hands and trust, trust, trust."

Rodleigh had never read anything like this before. He looked out the window over the fairgrounds, turning it over in his mind. Catching. Dying. After rereading the passage several times, he put the book on the shelf with their other Henri books, and went to tell Jennie about it.

"What Henri wrote about us in his book is not religious exactly, but about something much more free, about how the spirit can fly," he told her.

Jennie was intrigued. "So while we thought you were just teaching him a new vocabulary of circus and trapeze terms, it turns out you were also giving Henri a new vision of his faith?"

"And even more, just like we experiment with new routines in our trapeze act, Henri is experimenting with these new images in his books and sermons," reflected Rodleigh. "It's fun to think about. I wonder if it has been as exciting and daring for him as it is for us doing our work."

27

Rodleigh was right: Henri was experimenting, finding his voice in daring new ways as he tried to communicate the insights stimulated by their friendship.

Soon after Rodleigh received Henri's book, Henri was in Minneapolis, smiling as he fingered the new medal on a wide red ribbon around his neck. The medal recognized Henri's contributions to the international movement of spiritual and pastoral care and counseling. Through the lengthy standing ovation that followed the presentation of the medal, he looked thoughtfully over all those attending the meetings of COMISS (Coalition On Ministry In Specialized Settings), weighing what to say in response.

Speaking without notes, he began by describing his friendship with Adam. But he also wanted to say more about community, so he began to share his experience of the Flying Rodleighs.

"I love these trapeze artists a lot!" he exclaimed. *"There are three flyers and two catchers. Three flyers who make these incredible triples, you know."* In his eagerness to communicate the momentum of the act, Henri rotated his arms vigorously to demonstrate, setting his COMISS medal

swinging and nearly dislodging his microphone. *"Better be careful here,"* he admonished himself, and his audience laughed.

I wonder if they realize that the catcher doesn't just wait for the flyer? Henri thought. Before getting to know the Flying Rodleighs, he had no idea of the complex dynamics of the act, the constant split-second decisions and adjustments made by each artist. How can I help them to imagine the attentive teamwork required when everyone is already in motion? He tried to embody the momentum, swinging his right arm to illustrate. *"The catcher is on a catch bar that moves. Meanwhile the flyer comes from the pedestal and does all these triples."* Henri swiveled his left hand high above him, and swung it down to meet his right hand flying in from his right side. When his right hand caught his left wrist, both in motion, Henri looked triumphant and the audience laughed and applauded Henri's successful act.

"And Rodleigh says, 'Henri, you know the greatest temptation for me as a flyer is to try to catch the catcher. Because the catcher will be there. I have to trust that. When I come down from my triple I have to stretch out my hands, and whether I'm here"—Henri paused to turn, stretching his arms out—*"or whether I'm there"*—Henri pivoted slightly—*"or whether I'm here"*—he shifted his body's direction yet again—*"I have to trust that he will be there."* Henri demonstrated, again locking one hand over his other arm in trapeze catching action. *"And will pull me right up into the cupola."* Henri jubilantly swung his right arm in a high arc.

"That's what I have to trust. And if I start"—Henri opted to use gestures rather than words, reaching his arms in front of him while stumbling and turning confusedly—*"then we break our wrists and we are in trouble."*

Henri's audience of ministers and caregivers again leapt to their feet to applaud his performance of trust and teamwork in motion.

A FEW MONTHS EARLIER, Henri had received an invitation to address the National Catholic HIV/AIDS Ministry conference in Chicago. By 1994, AIDS had become the leading cause of death among all people aged twenty-five to forty-four in the United States.

When the invitation from the conference organizers arrived, Henri could not decide. He said yes, then changed his mind and declined. He felt confused by whether he was the right person to address such a gathering. He worried about how much of a toll it would take on him personally. But his connection with the Flying Rodleighs was giving him not only new ideas but courage to leap into something new and risky. Henri agreed to go to the conference and give the closing address.

As Henri prepared to give his talk at the end of the conference, he was nervous. It had been a good week, but he took a deep breath and wiped his sweaty hands on his corduroy trousers as he looked out over hundreds of people and announced:

> *I am really very grateful for being here this whole week. As a beginning of my sharing with you I would just tell you in a way how it all came about. In 1981 the founder of the community of L'Arche—it is a community for and with people with mental handicaps—I had never met him before, but he looked at me when we met and he realized that I was not terribly happy, and sort of anxious, and looking for something new. But I didn't know what it was and he said, "Maybe our people have a home for you. Maybe our people have something for you that you really need." It took me quite a while to listen to that, and it was in 1986 that I finally left the academic world and joined the community of L'Arche. And my life has been*

very, very different, radically different since I got there, frighteningly different.

In 1991 or '2, I met another man called Rodney DiMartini [the executive director of the National Catholic AIDS Network] and he looked at me and thought I wasn't looking very happy.

This got a laugh from Henri's audience, and so he bravely continued:

And he thought I might be a little anxious about certain things, certainly about some of the things that he was interested in.

Henri's audience applauded, and Henri grinned back at them.

He said, "Henri, maybe our people have something that you really need." It's quite humbling to always walk into people who tell you that they think that you need something.

So it took me a few years and finally I said well maybe. But first I said no, and then I said yes, and then I said no, and he said you better say yes finally, and so I'm here.

Being in this conference has been a little bit like a new jump into something unknown—a little bit frighteningly unknown and not knowing what it will do to me.

Encouraged by the responsive audience, Henri tried to explain the growth that he was experiencing:

Maybe my whole life has been a life in which boundaries were pushed out and broken down, and it has been frightening for me every time a new boundary came tumbling down. So I've realized okay I might have started in community or in the Church or in the seminary or in my family as a safe clear place, and then bang, bang, bang, bang, bang all these boundaries keep falling, all these little hedges and fences keep falling away. Suddenly, the non-believer might be more believing than the believer, the outsider might have something to teach the insider. Suddenly, the difference between Catholic and Protestant, Christian and Buddhist, religious and secular isn't the kind of difference I thought it was.

When I went to Daybreak, my community now, I realized that the difference between handicapped and non-handicapped just wasn't there anymore. I realized that I could love the handicapped only because I was handicapped, that I could be close to people in pain only because somehow they revealed my own pain to me.

The difference between male and female, young and old, married and celibate, White and persons of color—all the distinctions that seemed so important—suddenly the pandemic throws all those differences away—the difference between homosexual and asexual and bisexual people, or between married people and transgender people—I've never heard so many terms!

Henri's audience applauded and cheered.

It seems that these differences aren't that important actually. Married, celibate, single—you can be anything but we are together, the AIDS pandemic brings us together. I tell you that for me personally, and I would guess in some places for you, that when the boundaries are falling away you get anxious sometimes and say "now where do I say stop or here, here, this is it?" And it's no longer there and suddenly you realize that your heart is expanding and there are no boundaries to that expansion.

Henri continued, talking about the paradox he had experienced, that love and intimacy in community can unexpectedly reveal a deeper inner loneliness. But sorrow and joy are not separate, they are always in our flesh, Henri asserted boldly, so *"just start living!"*

Studying the responses of the many new friends he had met over the week, Henri decided to tell them about the Flying Rodleighs. He made it dramatic.

> *I have a little story to tell at the end of these reflections. A few years ago, my eighty-eight-year-old father came to visit me in Germany. He wanted to do something fun, so I said, "Let's go to the circus."*
>
> *There were five South African trapeze artists—they left the pedestals and danced in the air and I said to my father, "I think I missed my vocation! That's what I always wanted. That's what I always wanted to do. To fly!"*
>
> *I said, "You go look to the animals in the break, but I'm going to talk to these artists." And I said, "Hey guys you are absolutely fabulous"—and I was this sixteen-year-old fan looking at these strong and big thirty-year-old guys.*
>
> *They said, "Well, do you want to come to our practice tomorrow?" And I said, "YES! I want to come to your practice tomorrow!"*

Henri's audience whooped as he acted out the scene he was describing. Looking out over people who were daily facing so much death, Henri ached to inspire and encourage them. The spiritual meaning of flying and catching was not just about death, he realized, but about living, about the remarkable community he had experienced that week in the National Catholic HIV/AIDS Ministry conference and saw embodied in front of him. The catcher offered an image for dying, but it was also about the beauty and artistry of flying and catching each other day by day.

There was that moment that he couldn't get out of his mind, when the flyer had to let go of everything and fly in midair, trusting that the catcher would be there at the precise moment when most needed. All that week, Henri had listened to how everybody at the conference was involved in that act, disciplined in their love, risking, letting go, trusting, and catching each other. This was the crucial thing he had learned from Rodleigh.

The only thing I have to do, Rodleigh said, is stretch out my hands. After I've done my thing—stretch out and trust, trust that he will be there, and pull me right back up.

We have to love one another for that kind of trust. You and I are doing a lot of flying and I wish we do a lot more of it, and a lot of jumping and a lot of saltos and I hope we can do a few triples. It's wonderful to see and you will get a lot of applause and it's good. Enjoy it! But finally it's trust—trust, when you come down from your triple, know that the catcher will be there.

The audience was silent for a beat, taking in this image, then applauded for a long time.

28

In a hallway of the Hotel Lapershoek, Henri has lost all sense of time. How long has he been traveling? He realizes that his journey has entered a new phase when his stretcher stops. He can feel a cool breeze.

Through the large, open window, Dennie greets the firefighter standing in the basket handling the controls of the basket and the boom. Henri with his head toward the window cannot see him, so Dennie explains to Henri what will happen next.

"We will rest the stretcher on the window frame. There is someone at the controls of the basket who will help guide the stretcher safely into place. You will go headfirst out of the window."

Headfirst. Henri vaguely wonders if he has always gone head-first. All his life, his father has liked intelligent people and encouraged Henri to pursue the life of the mind. But in this moment there is no separation between his thinking and his body—like it or not, his whole body is coming out a window. He is well wrapped in his sheet and blanket, with straps now securing him to his stretcher. Dennie's voice and presence comfort him. He is not alone.

The firefighters carefully push his stretcher out over the windowsill toward the basket on the aerial lift. His head is suddenly in the open air. The stretcher slides with a metallic scrape onto the rail along the bottom of the platform in the basket. Dennie stands at his feet, still on the other side of the window opening. Henri looks over and sees the firefighter who is controlling the basket. He nods at Henri, then crouches down to work with Dennie to bring the stretcher into its final position and anchor it. Henri feels it click into place.

"You are attached safely now," says Dennie as he climbs out the window into the basket beside Henri. "There is nothing for you to do." The stretcher feels solid, but the whole situation is unsettling. Dennie seems to guess what Henri is thinking. "I am here with you," he adds reassuringly.

The day is cloudy and the breeze on Henri's face is fresh. He is really in the air now. Henri blinks nearsightedly at the gray clouds overhead. He tries to remember his words about trust in his letter to Bart Gavigan:

> *One of the parts of the act that deeply moves me is the long jump. In that act the flyer flies across the whole span of the circus, with out-stretched arms and hands, to be caught by the catcher on the moving catch bar. The words that really struck me were the words by Rod-leigh, "When I have done my flying, I have to stretch out my hands, and trust that the catcher will be there for me. The greatest mistake I can make is to try to catch the catcher." I have thought about these words as words that express the human challenge to trust your neighbor, to trust your God, to trust love, to trust that finally we will be safe.*

He closes his eyes, and his mind floats away again.

.••••.

By the summer of 1994, Henri decided that the best way to engage an audience would be a filmed documentary with the Flying Rodleighs. Looking back, his excitement had been inspired not by their words, but because he saw them perform. Maybe to understand what he wanted to communicate, an audience would need to see them. *The Flying Rodleighs are a trapeze group that communicates through the body. Their act is wordless, but in the wordless communication they create community. Children, young people, and old people, from all different backgrounds and nationalities can be together in watching their flying and catching.*

Over months, Henri and Bart explored and discussed the film. Jan van den Bosch in Holland was interested in producing it. Bart confirmed that he would direct it, and also write and edit an English-language version.

Of course, Henri also discussed the idea with Rodleigh and the troupe. The Flying Rodleighs were flattered but somewhat bewildered at the prospect of being featured in a film made for a religious channel.

On December 23, 1994, filming began at the Ahoy Sports Centre in Rotterdam. Jan and Bart started the interview with Rodleigh outside, but it was so cold that after a few minutes Rodleigh was unable to enunciate his words. Henri arrived in the afternoon with a big hug and delight beyond words—he just stood grinning at his friends.

Henri's friend Jan interviewed him for the film, asking, "When you describe a situation, if it's faith, or *The Prodigal Son*, or *In the Name of Jesus*, all your best-sellers, you write very intensely about it. What will happen with this story?"

"I don't know," Henri admitted. *"You know I've always tried to write about deep human experiences."*

Jan pressed his point. "Is this too difficult to write about?"

Maybe. I've tried to write about Latin America. I've tried to write about living with the Trappist monks. I have tried to write about intimate things like my mother's death. But I've known the Rodleighs for four years and I still really don't know how to write about it, as if it touches something so deep in me that I'm not yet able to know how to express it. It's even something different than writing about Rembrandt. I mean, this is something totally new for me. Not just that the trapeze is new. What they represent is new. The experience in me of the trapeze—that's new—and I don't even know yet if I ever will be able to give words to it or write a book about it.

Henri became even more animated. How could he communicate his excitement to a viewing audience?

You know, when I got to know the Rodleighs a lot better, I also realized that they are not an ideal family. No family is ideal. They have conflict, they have struggles. They have difficulties—bodily, mentally, spiritually. They are just people like we are. But one of the things they said to me, you know, when you go on the trapeze, forget everything else. Be only there and be totally there.

So here we are, people full of conflicts, difficulties, worries, concerns, guilt feelings, hopes, all that, but somehow the ability to be totally present in the present—that creates kind of a glimpse of eternity, gives you a glimpse of the true life. You certainly know what real beauty is, or real harmony is, or real unity is—something that your heart most desires—for a second.

·····

PERCHED NOW ATOP THE medical lift in the open air, Henri wonders for a moment how precarious his present situation is. Yet he can't help remembering what he said about risk in the film interview: *We all want to make triples and doubles and layouts and double doubles and all of these things. We like to take risks. We like to be free in the air, in life. But you have to know there's a catcher. We have to know that when we come down from it all, we're going to be caught, we're going to be safe.*

"Henri, trust the catcher!" he reminds himself now.

•••••

THE FILMING WAS COMPLETED and on New Year's Day 1995, Henri came with nearly his entire Dutch family to see the show and bid his friends farewell. He was in a good mood. He gave each of the Flying Rodleighs a heartfelt hug before dancing off along the canals of Rotterdam with his niece Laura. The troupe's final days in Holland were unusually quiet without Henri and they sat after each show reflecting on the whole experience of filming and meeting his family, wondering when they would see him again. Henri had announced that he would be taking a sabbatical later in 1995 to try to complete the book about them.

The Rodleighs received Bart's completed English-language video, titled *Angels Over the Net*, in early July 1995. Its effect surprised them. They listened to Henri's explanation:

> *Now I live and work with people with mental handicaps, and some also have severe physical handicaps. One of the things that has struck me in my life was that the people with a physical and mental handicap are quite often very able to create community.*

I live in a community with people from twenty-one different nations. Some people are married, some people are single, some people are old, some people are young, some people are Japanese, some Brazilian—and normally these people would never form community, but in the middle of them there are people with a weak body who often can't even speak, who can't express themselves in ideas or big discussions yet still these people are able to create a community among people who otherwise would never live well together.

For me, this is a really new discovery. You know, first I taught. I loved to teach in the university. Then I felt I missed something, something of the heart. So I discovered the life of handicapped people. It was a real discovery and the handicapped people became also my teachers, the teachers of the heart. While they can't speak, while they cannot explain, they tell me something. They tell me that being is more important than doing. They tell me that the heart is more important than the mind. They tell me that community is more important than doing things alone. All these great valuable truths these handicapped people taught me without any words.

When I saw the Rodleighs, I saw in a way the same thing. I saw people who don't speak on the trapeze, who do something with their bodies, and who create community first of all among themselves as a little group, and among all these people who come to see them—young people, old people, children, people from all different languages. They all understand—they create family wherever they go. They bring people together.

As Rodleigh watched the video and showed it to others, he began to see their performance and his own responsibility from a new viewpoint. He had never thought of their work as a form of community or even communication with the audience, but now he was touched by the response of people watching the video. He wiped a tear from his cheek. He was not alone; he knew that many others responded in the same way. Henri had confided that he too shed tears each time he watched it.

29

In the summer of 1995, Henri was invited back to speak at the next National Catholic HIV/AIDS Ministry conference. He was surprised by how anxious he felt. He worried about whether he had anything more to offer. But he said yes. His friends Sue Mosteller and Kathy Bruner came with him.

This conference would be bigger, and there had been thousands more deaths in the year since the last conference. Just a month earlier, the American Food and Drug Administration had approved the first antiretroviral treatment for HIV, but there was no treatment for AIDS in sight and the epidemic was exploding. Millions of people had died worldwide.

The gathering began with an interpretive dance. The audience stood in a single large floor space. Many people packed the space, crammed in closely to watch the dancers as they held each other close and let each other go, honoring all those who had died of AIDS. Henri and those around him wept openly.

The dance drew people together into a community like the artistry of the circus, Henri reflected as he dried his eyes. Like the Flying Rodleighs, here were performers who did not speak and had tremendous power to unite people. Living art, in motion and time, creating community.

When Henri got up to speak partway through the conference, he was again both nervous and moved by his audience. He prayed that he would find the right words. This time Henri boldly titled his talk "Befriending Death."

He talked about his friend Peter, who was dying with AIDS. Peter's partner was insisting, *"He won't die—we will fight it!"* while Peter was saying, *"Why me? I have spent my life serving God—I am confused and angry and frustrated."*

Henri explained that he was struck by this: the partner wanted to combat the illness as a warrior, while Peter's voice was the voice of a protester, the voice of resistance. After spending time with them, Henri wondered, *"What is the way here? Is there a way that my friend and his partner can go one more step and embrace the truth of their reality? Can they befriend death that stands in their room and say, 'Yes you are my enemy but I am called to love my enemy and I want to love you. I want to be with you without fear'?"*

"Why was it so hard for them to become lovers of their enemy death?" Henri asked.

He recounted for his audience how he had thought through that question, then realized that his friends were afraid that if they started embracing death, Peter would die sooner. In other words, to start thinking about death would be to give up and no longer resist.

Henri asked the audience, *"Is it possible to love and resist? If we are called to love our enemies, then we must be able to both love and resist at the same time."*

The embodied power of love can make people better resisters,

Henri suggested. *"You must claim your spiritual truth while everything around us suggests disclaimers. It has to come right from your gut, right from your center, right from your heart."*

Describing his own experience in 1989 when he was hit by the van and nearly died, Henri remembered, *"When I was close to death, I experienced one thing: I didn't want to die alone."* But, Henri added, no human being *"can finally give us the spiritual power to make that passage. My deepest conviction is that what allows us to make that passage finally is the communion of saints."* He pointed his listeners to *"that incredible spiritual family that surrounds you and makes your exodus possible,"* and *"that family that reaches out beyond the boundaries of birth and death."*

> *You belong to all the people who went before you. You have to embrace them as saints. Yes, those who were born and died long ago struggled like me and were anguished like me. They had their sexual struggles as I have, and they were lonely and depressed and confused. They went through the black plague. They are part of my human family. I see this crowd of witnesses that I belong to.*

·····

SUSPENDED IN MIDAIR OUTSIDE the hotel, for the first time it occurs to Henri that he could die. He hasn't really let that thought enter his mind before. Having survived when the van mirror hit him, he has assumed he will continue living for a long time. His father is well into his nineties. Henri has never imagined the possibility of dying before his father.

But sometimes, thinks Henri, you just have to let go, even if in that moment you are not sure who is your catcher. Maybe it takes a whole lifetime to learn how to fly, and how to fall. He opens his eyes to see the treetops and rooftops of Hilversum, but without his glasses, Dennie and the entire situation feel out of focus. He closes his eyes again.

He is no longer in much pain, but the thoughts swirling in his mind feel urgent and intensely personal. What would allow him to die well? Henri wonders. He has written and spoken a lot about this in the past few years, but the question is now lodged in his own body with shocking immediacy.

> You were the beloved before you were born, and you will be the beloved after you die. That's the truth of your identity. That's who you are whether you feel bad or not bad, or whatever the world makes you think or experience. You belong to God from eternity to eternity. Life is just an interruption of eternity, just a little opportunity for a few years to say, "I love you, too."

Dying would be a very understandable reason to leave his trapeze book incomplete, a permanent interruption, he thinks. Maybe he has already learned everything he needs from the trapeze.

> When I met the Rodleighs and I saw their work and I got to know the trapeze world, again something really new happened. It was suddenly as if I discovered the incredible message the body can give. You know, it was like the university was the mind, L'Arche was the heart, but the trapeze was about the body. And the body tells a spiritual story.

V

Flying

30

Dennie studies Henri, trying to gauge whether the tension in his body is pain, anxiety, or something else entirely. All he has to work with is what he observes in Henri's physical reactions. Henri's body is certainly telling a story, Dennie thinks, but he wonders how much he is missing of Henri's experience. He notes how inwardly focused Henri seems to be. Henri is a priest, so maybe he is having deep spiritual reflections. Perhaps he is praying. But he needs to stay in his body until they get him to the hospital. Dennie's warm hand cups Henri's shoulder reassuringly.

.....

HENRI SET THE NEW hardcover journal on the desk in front of him. After admiring the cover's bright detail of Claude Monet's *Bouquet of Sunflowers*, he opened to the first lined page and began: *Oakville, Ontario, Saturday, September 2, 1995. This is the first day of my sabbatical. I am excited and anxious, hopeful and fearful, tired, and full of desire to do a thousand things.*

A year of freedom, *completely open to let something radically new happen,* Henri exulted. *I feel strange! Very happy and very scared at the same time. . . . Free to deepen friendships and explore new ways of loving. Free most of all to fight with the Angel of God and ask for a new blessing.*

On Friday, September 8, he continued, *I have written many essays, reflections, and meditations during the last twenty-five years. But I have seldom written a good story. Why not? Maybe my moralistic nature made me focus more on the uplifting message that I felt compelled to proclaim than on the often ambiguous realities of daily life, from where any uplifting message has to emerge spontaneously. Maybe I have been afraid to touch the wet soil from which new life comes forth and anxious about the outcome of an open-ended story.*

THREE MONTHS LATER IN early December, while staying with friends in Massachusetts, Henri went with his hosts to see the American Repertory Theater's production of *The Tempest.*

By the end of the play I was mesmerized by its magical power, Henri wrote. *Prospero, the exiled Duke of Milan, brooding about revenge, ends up embracing all his enemies.*

Not only that, Henri noted, but Prospero speaks directly to the audience in an epilogue. Henri was so moved by it that he searched out the precise passage and carefully transcribed it into his journal in his graceful handwriting:

> *And my ending is despair,*
> *Unless I be relieved by prayer,*
> *Which pierces so that it assaults*
> *Mercy itself and frees all faults.*

As you from crimes would pardoned be,
Let your indulgence set me free.

Henri stopped to consider why this moved him so much. Maybe because the question of how to turn enemies into friends had been with him his entire life. He had, after all, grown up in Europe during World War II. He remembered those years of political conflict as he considered Prospero's transformation, then turned his thoughts inward to his own lifelong quest to make his tumultuous, passionate interior life into a friend, not an enemy.

Just a few months earlier, Henri had suggested to people at the AIDS conference that in the end, the challenge for every person is to befriend death itself. *The Tempest* was Shakespeare's last play, he noted, and continued writing: *After this he retired to Stratford and died four years later on April 23, 1616. Thus the final words of Prospero get a special meaning: Shakespeare asking his public to free him by their forgiveness.*

There are three old men here, Henri thought: Prospero, Shakespeare, and himself, all looking for forgiveness and the opportunity to launch out and become more free.

He sat with this idea for a while, then finished his journal entry. *For myself, I want to remember the famous words:*

How many goodly creatures are there here!
How beauteous mankind is! O brave new world
that has such people in't.

Less than two weeks later, Henri chuckled to himself, remembering those words as he flew into yet another beauteous new world.

31

A snowstorm was closing in on Signature Aviation in Boston's Logan International Airport as Joan Kroc's private Gulfstream jet, the Impromptu IV, waited to take off. Henri was already on board, roaming around full of excitement, admiring his friend Joan's elegantly equipped plane, touring the cockpit and meeting the crew. Sue Mosteller's flight from Toronto was late, but she arrived in time for a swift deicing of the plane and off they flew to pick up Fred and Joanne Rogers in Pittsburgh, then another friend of Joan's in Minneapolis.

The next morning, Henri and Sue spoke about "a spirituality of care" to about a hundred people gathered at the twenty-four-room hospice in San Diego.

A large portrait of Joan in the entrance hall celebrates her as the founder and mega-donor of this remarkable place. The staff is very gentle and friendly and the atmosphere is homey and quite intimate. Both Sue and I spoke about preparing ourselves and others for "dying well." We sang some Taize songs and had a very lively exchange with the audience. We all felt quite uplifted by the event.

Henri and Joan had met the year before and immediately become friends. They had a lot in common. Joan was a gifted musician who for years had worked as a professional pianist. She intuitively understood Henri's experience of the artistry of the trapeze performance.

Joan's social situation touched Henri. She was the heir of her late husband Ray Kroc's fortune. Over his years at Yale and Harvard then Daybreak, Henri developed a concern for the spiritual struggles of people who were very wealthy. In 1992, he observed, *My experience is that rich people are also poor, but in other ways. Many rich people are very lonely. Many struggle with a sense of being used. Others suffer from feelings of rejection or depression.*

Henri liked how Joan's creative mind was always thinking about how to make life better for all kinds of people, people who lacked adequate housing, people who were dying. He was moved by how she talked about children as the future and wanted every child, no matter their circumstances, to live up to their potential.

Henri also agreed wholeheartedly with Joan's commitment to a more peaceful world, and was intrigued by her insistence that the way to world peace was through education, especially helping women around the world to develop and take up leadership in all levels of society.

Just before 6 p.m., Henri looked in his mirror, smoothed his unruly gray hair, and strolled out to join around ninety guests who had arrived from across the country for a party.

A large tent had been set up with thousands of little lights. All around the pool round tables were placed with splendid bouquets of white flowers. A tree full of lights was floating in the pool. He admired the large stars hung in the biggest trees. Red and white lights adorned the entrance road and hedges. Most dramatic were the sculptures in the garden, illuminated by carefully placed floodlights.

The surroundings were spectacular, the food delicious, the conversations friendly, the music pleasant and everything very, very elegant. Joan wore an all-gold long dress. She told me that she had bought that dress long ago and never had a chance to wear it. "So I planned a party, to have a chance to show my dress," she said jokingly.

By 10 p.m., most guests had left and I went to bed, somewhat dazzled, puzzled, and intrigued by the life I had been part of.

The next day, after *a lively conversation on the meaning of Advent,* Joan's houseguests toured a homeless shelter that she helped support. Henri was impressed by the scope of the project, but left wondering about the relationships he had seen. *Where and how are the homeless people offering their gifts? Where is there any mutuality between giver and receiver?*

After we had returned to Joan's estate, we celebrated the Eucharist together in the garden in front of the Mexican creche, with figures larger than life. We sat around the little table, read the readings, shared our reflections, prayed and received the sacred gifts of the Body and Blood of Christ.

At the end of the Eucharist we walked over to the new statue that Joan had recently acquired. Joan asked me to bless it. It is a huge bronze sculpture of a seated Cardinal, made by the Italian artist Giacomo Manzù.

Henri and Joan both loved art. Her new sculpture captivated him, with its clean-shaven, ageless face. The expression was solemn, but the left ear was tucked under the Cardinal's tall miter while the right ear stuck out. It seemed a tender detail, a moment of listening, affirming the humanity of the majestic Cardinal.

Henri packed quickly the next morning, and they all drove back to the airport to board Joan's plane. Henri's friend Robert Jonas picked him up at the airport in Boston.

"How was it?" he asked. I said, "I don't even know how to talk about it. It's like leaving the atmosphere and entering a space where the normal laws of gravity no longer count."

Perhaps, he mused, Joan's world was a bit like the flying trapeze, which also performed seemingly without the limitations of gravity. She and her friends traveled in a world of wealth and power, and yet her situation required its own kind of artistry.

When Henri sat down to write a thank-you letter to Joan, he wanted to offer her something more than just thanks. Thinking of Joan's generosity and social vision, Henri wrote, *Unconditional love is love without conditions, without strings attached, without prerequisites, without demands. It is giving without expecting anything in return.*

He paused and thought about this. Love offered for its own sake. Maybe that too was rather like the trapeze, a performance for its own sake. He thought about something he had said in his taped comments after meeting the Flying Rodleighs. *But when you see these trapeze artists, it becomes a symbol. What do these people do? They fly through the air and they want to do a highly skilled, safe, and entertaining act. They want to do it well and although they're terribly happy when people admire them, there is a kind of "l'art pour l'art."*

Henri carried on with his letter to Joan:

> *This unconditional love is the love that Jesus calls us to "love your enemies and do good to them and lend without any hope of return. You will have a great reward and you will be children of the Most High, for he himself is kind to the ungrateful and the wicked"*

(Luke 6:32–35). Is this a human possibility? It sounds completely unrealistic. Isn't giving without receiving a set-up for burnout?

The answer is quite simple. No, it is not impossible to love unconditionally because we are loved unconditionally! God loved us before we were born, and God will still love us after we have died.

Henri again paused in his writing. He thought about Prospero's swing from decades of plotting revenge to embracing his enemies in mercy. And then Prospero directly engaged the audience, shedding his magical cloak and sharing his vulnerability. Henri recalled his artistic, musical friend Joan in her dazzling gold dress and smiled at the comparison. How could he help a very public, even magical figure like Joan trust enough to give and receive unconditional love?

The Flying Rodleighs had given him an image for the arc of risk and trust that is the shape of each human life, Henri reflected. Ultimately, each person belongs to God and will return to God. But flying is done together, as a troupe of human beings. He chewed his pencil and looked out the window at the cloudy winter sky. Sometimes people are ungrateful or even wicked, as he had just written to Joan. Sometimes people are careless or incompetent or afraid. Everyone makes mistakes. He thought again of Rodleigh's insistence that each member of the troupe honestly assess each performance, criticizing each other, identifying what went wrong, and affirming all that worked well. Then they wrapped themselves in their shiny performance capes to begin the next show with confidence and trust, without carrying resentment or fear. *I was fascinated by their dedication, by their discipline, by the way they worked together, by their kindness to each other, by the whole way in which they did things,* he noted at the time.

He continued his letter, trying to expand for Joan this understanding of unconditional love:

> It is not a sentimental, all approving, and always agreeing love. It can even be a confronting love. But it is unconditional! Unconditional love, therefore, does not include approval of everything the person we love does.
>
> It is not always easy to believe that we can be unconditionally loved even when those who love us disagree with us or disapprove of us. But this is the love with which God loves us and wants us to love each other.

32

During the first few months of his sabbatical, Henri went to two different circuses. The first was the "Greatest Show on Earth" in the United States.

>*I was so bombarded with all that was going on in front of me, that I could hardly tolerate it. Glitter, glamour, and excitement! But what to do with it all?*
>
>*This afternoon I was impressed, overwhelmed, awestruck etc., but never really moved. There was one moment when I got "caught." It was when Vasili Zinoviev performed a one armed handstand on the head of his partner Pavel Karime, who keeps two freestanding stilts in balance on a platform 30 feet above the arena floor.*
>
>*I could see them so well since our seats were right in front of the act. Vasili's open smile and his beautiful muscular body radiated so much vitality and joyful energy and joy that, for a moment, I felt personally connected with him and would have liked to know him and his partner. But then they vanished in the large anonymity of the show.*

It was an important moment for me, short as it was. I recognized within me the same emotions that "caught" me when I first saw the Flying Rodleighs. It was the emotion that made me take the risk of introducing myself to them and that led to a long and rich friendship. Vasili and Pavel were like a flash of light in the darkness, a recognition, a memory, and an inner connection full of melancholy.

In late December, Henri and his father were visiting Freiburg together. Recalling seeing Circus Barum together five years earlier, Henri's father suggested, "There is a circus in town again. Would you like to go?" It was the Christmas Circus Festival featuring the Chinese People's circus with guest artists from Moscow and Paris.

Spectacular as it was, nothing happened to me comparable to what happened five years ago. Then I was "hooked" by the Rodleighs and felt really driven to see them again and again and enter deeply into their world. Now I saw a good show and went home without many after thoughts or after feelings. Then I saw something that opened in me a new inner place. Now I just enjoyed some unusual sights. Then I experienced a personal transformation. Now I had a few hours of good entertainment.

A FEW DAYS LATER, Henri was overjoyed to receive an unexpected phone call from Rodleigh.

"Where are you?" I said.
"We are in Zwolle," he said, "and we have been trying to reach you ever since we came to Holland. Can you come to visit us?"

I was so excited to hear from my friends. The last time I saw them was a year ago when we made the documentary which was shown on Dutch TV.

On Sunday, January 7, I was sitting with Rodleigh and his wife, Jennie, in their caravan. Soon I also saw Jon, Kail, Karlene, and Slava. It felt so good to see them all again. I realized how much I had missed being with them.

Rodleigh told me about their hard times, very complicated problems with their caravans, serious health problems, and most of all the death of Raedawn, Rodleigh's and Karlene's sister, in Italy. Listening to all of it I was amazed that the Flying Rodleighs hadn't canceled any performances and had been able to continue to work on their tricks.

Jennie had stopped working in the acts but Kerri, a sixteen-year-old from South Africa, had been trained to take her place.

The Rodleighs performed poorly. Because of the low ceiling of the hall the whole act had been toned down and the two most spectacular tricks failed. Both Slava and Rodleigh missed their catcher and ended up on the net.

Between the act of the Flying Rodleighs and "the finale," we had tea with Karlene and Jon. Since my last visit Karlene and Jon have fallen in love and become a couple. Karlene's daughter was happy to have a real family now. We had a very good and lively visit.

The reunion was a joy. After the year's absence, Henri had settled in for the short visit as if he had been living with them for the whole year, though Rodleigh noted with concern how exhausted Henri looked, and Henri admitted that his year's sabbatical was more tiring than his usual work.

Driving back to the circus after taking their visitors to the train station, Rodleigh pondered how their five-year friendship had evolved. The year since they had last been together had been painful. When Rodleigh and Karlene's sister died that year, Rodleigh especially missed Henri and wished Henri lived closer to be with him in his grief.

It's strange, thought Rodleigh, he still felt mystified by Henri's desire to write about them. The video helped, but in personal terms, there was something more than the video captured. Thinking about it, Rodleigh tried to puzzle out each element, in the same way that he methodically worked out each move of a complicated new act.

Rodleigh turned back into the fairgrounds and jumped out of the car, wondering if Henri's need for community was satisfied in their troupe because they accepted him without trying to change him. Not that trying to change him would have worked anyway, Rodleigh chuckled, remembering the muddy feet. But something about the flamboyant and marginalized world of the circus felt like home to Henri, as it did to Rodleigh. Every day the troupe dealt with crises and failures, then continued to perform. Perhaps Henri's spiritual life was similar to the daily challenges facing us in our circus life, thought Rodleigh.

Jennie had a pot of tea ready.

"Sometimes I think that Henri desperately wants to be accepted, especially by God. I'm sure it's more than just a boyhood fantasy to perform as a flyer that attracted him to our act," Rodleigh commented. "Maybe we were the ingredients he needed to clarify certain feelings. I think that he sees in us a visual representation of his spiritual feelings, something that he feels within himself."

Jennie poured two cups of tea and handed one to Rodleigh. "What do you think he sees?"

Rodleigh sipped his tea. "We always want to perform a perfect act but we often fail. Do you think that we showed Henri something about overcoming the fear of failure? In a way, he could imagine climbing the ladder with us to try again, even with everyone watching. I think that he learned to identify with us by taking risks and testing his limits."

"Also, all of us have to forget everything else and concentrate on just one thing for a short time. That's how he tried to describe his idea of prayer," Jennie remembered.

Rodleigh grinned. "So we can say that we gave Henri courage as he danced dangerously through the air!"

They gulped back the last of their hot drinks, threw on their track suits, and hurried across the fairgrounds to prepare for the second performance, still wondering why Henri had not been able to begin writing his book.

In Utrecht, Holland, later that evening, Henri completed his journal entry:

> As I reflected on this short visit I realized how good it had been for me. I am really looking forward to being with them again in June or July—and to realize my long dream to write a book about them. I experienced a new energy to write about the Flying Rodleighs in ways that they themselves could appreciate.

33

Henri celebrated his sixty-fourth birthday on Wednesday, January 24, with just his father. They watched the *Angels Over the Net* video about the Flying Rodleighs and Henri's father loved it. Because the heating system did not work, they huddled by the open fire, *two old men sitting close to the fireplace warming their hands.*

Henri continued his journal entry:

I feel happy today. Grateful to God and my family and friends for all the graces that have come to me during these 64 years. I look forward to the years to come as years to deepen my life with God and my friendship with people.

I especially hope that I will have more space and time to write. Deep in myself I feel that something new wants to be born: a book with stories, a novel, a spiritual journal—something quite different from what I have done in the past.

MEANWHILE, HENRI AND HIS editor, Bill Barry at Doubleday in New York, had agreed that his "secret journal" from his breakdown in 1987–88 would be published in September 1996. Henri felt both curious and wary diving back into this record of the worst period of his life. How much had he grown through those terrible months? Although he had gained more perspective in the intervening years, he still felt *a certain fear about working on the manuscript. Maybe I am afraid to reenter the extremely painful experience.*

Reviewing his early journal entries from his time of therapy, he came across affirmations spoken to him by his therapists: *Trust, trust that God will give you that all-fulfilling love and will give it to you in a human way. Before you die God will offer you the deepest satisfaction you can desire. Just stop running and start trusting and receiving. You need human hands to hold you there.* That reminded him of discovering the Flying Rodleighs, and growing to understand the trust required between the human hands of flyers and catchers.

The trapeze could become a story of redemption, of resurrection, Henri reflected, but then he stopped. He didn't want to spiritualize it so quickly that the experience became disembodied.

> *The Flying Rodleighs teach me something about being in the body, being incarnate, being enfleshed. You know, the real spiritual life is an enfleshed life. So the Rodleighs are teaching me by who they are something more about what my deepest search really is all about.*

He knew his desire: to tell a true story about the body, and to affirm that story as spiritual, because the spirit is always embodied. But again he was stuck. What story about the body did he want to tell? What was the story of his own body?

As LONG AS HE could remember, Henri had longed to feel physically part of welcoming communities. Writing about the march from Selma, he had claimed that his hitchhiking friend Charles *was turning me into a Black man,* as Henri was shocked to experience a small bit of the exclusion and hatred that Charles lived with daily. The march itself was simultaneously unnerving and joyful.

> *I said to myself, "Yes, yes, I belong; these are my people. They may have differently-coloured skin, a different religion, a different way of life, but they are my brothers and sisters. They love me, and I love them. Their smiles and tears are my smiles and tears; their prayers and prophecies are my prayers and prophecies; their anguish and hope are my anguish and hope. I am one with them."*

Yet some of Henri's most terrifying experiences over the past decades had been when he had literally lost all sense of his own body's boundaries. It happened several times. After giving successful talks to thousands of people he felt himself physically dispersed and scattered. Friends remembered his desperate late-night phone calls or visits, begging them just to hold him until he felt that he was safe in his own body again.

Right from his early days in L'Arche back in 1986, when Henri lived in the Trosly community, he struggled with the very physical foundations of L'Arche relationships. At that time he was not responsible for the physical care of anyone, but the very idea of it unsettled him.

Thursday, March 20, 1986

Until now my whole life has been centered around the word: learning, teaching, reading, writing, speaking. Without the word my life is unthinkable.

L'Arche, however, is not built on words but on the body. Feeding, cleaning, touching, holding—this is what builds the community. Words are secondary. Most handicapped people have few words to speak, many do not speak at all. It is the language of the body that counts most.

"The Word became flesh." That is the center of the Christian message. Jesus confronts us with the word that can be seen, heard, and touched. The body thus becomes the way to know the word and to enter into relationship with the word.

I feel a deep resistance against this way.

When Henri arrived at Daybreak, Henri's friend Sue was amused to notice that he was uncomfortable hugging. It was like hugging a board, she teased him.

Did Henri almost envy Adam? As far as Henri could tell, Adam entrusted his body to Henri's care with no anxiety or self-consciousness.

My closeness to him and to his body was bringing me closer to myself and to my own body. My many words, spoken or written, always tempted me to go up into lofty ideas and perspectives without keeping in touch with the dailiness and beauty of ordinary life. Adam didn't allow this. It was as if he said to me, "Not only do you have a body like I do, Henri, but you are your body. Don't let your words become separated from your flesh. Your words must become and re-main flesh."

In the years after Henri's emotional break and his return to Day-break, he learned to hug. Sue noticed his tense body relaxing, first into trust, then opening out, widening into welcome and blessing.

At the National Catholic HIV/AIDS Ministry conference in the summer of 1994, Henri declared, *"Next I want to talk about the body, which is sort of a scary thing for me to talk about. The body was very much part of this conference."*

His audience laughed at the understatement. Henri continued:

> *What I have learned is that the body is indeed not just a metaphor, and that I've lived the body very much as a metaphor. I've been in-creasingly afraid to live in my body as a reality, as a real place of being.*
>
> *I don't even have the full words to know what this all means but I know somewhere that I have to really discover what it means to be a body, to be in the body, to be incarnate, to be the temple of the Spirit, to be at home in myself and therefore fully intimate with God because of that, at home in my home where God dwells.*
>
> *I've learned in the conference that there is not only one way, not a thousand ways, but more and more ways to be and live with the body.*

When the Flying Rodleighs burst into Henri's life, Henri suddenly found artistic, wordless expression of the body-centered spirituality he had been seeking. And his whole body yearned to participate: *"When I saw the Rodleighs for the first time I said I missed my vocation—I should have become a flyer. On the other hand, my body is as unpractical and unhandy as possible—but interiorly, spiritually, I realize I always would have liked to be a flyer."*

He marveled at how completely at home the Flying Rodleighs were in their physical interactions.

And then there was the intimacy thing. I must say, being caught— the catching is a wonderful image—catching another human being who is coming flying at you—to catch him so he doesn't fall in the net. It has very much of an intimate quality—you're protecting each other from falling.

Rodleigh was making enormous somersaults in the air, then Jon catches him just at the last minute before he goes down. Then suddenly there's this sense of "Wow, he's safe." Somebody is right there at the time you need him.

And Jon, too, hangs by his legs and he's making these swings, getting ready to catch somebody who is flying up to him—he's there to catch them, and they catch each other on the wrists; they don't catch each other on the hands—they sort of slide into each other's arms, but there's a kind of warmth there, a kind of safety, kind of a being held well. And, in fact, Jon and Karlene call their acts that they do right there at the top of the circus, cradling.

So that mutuality, being in touch with each other in that kind of way really speaks to me. And it's a very profound sort of feeling.

In a letter to Bart, Henri tried to express how he saw something spiritual in the bodies of his trapeze friends:

The Flying Rodleighs express some of the deepest human desires. The desire to fly freely, and the desire to be safely caught. The act in a way is an expression of the human spirit, as it is incarnate in the athletic bodies of the trapeze artists.

As Henri became more at home in his body, he raised with several editors the possibility of writing a book that would directly explore questions of sexuality. By the next summer, he mused to a journalist, *"Every human being lives a sexual life, whether you're celibate or married or whatever. Sexual life is life. That sexual life has to be lived as a life that deepens the communion with God and with our fellow human beings. And if it doesn't, then it can be very harmful. I haven't found the right language for it yet and hope I will one day."*

Gradually, Henri began to feel a little more free, even playful. Early in 1996, he amused some of his New York editors over an elegant lunch at the Barbetta restaurant by blurting out happily, *"Don't think that I don't want to have sex with everyone in this restaurant! I have fantasies just like everyone else!"* His editors stared in astonishment, looked speculatively around the restaurant, and then they all burst out laughing together with Henri.

34

Henri's secretary phoned him in New Jersey on February 12, 1996. "You need to come back to Daybreak today, Henri. Adam is dying." Within hours, Henri boarded a plane to Toronto to say goodbye. His words poured out into his journal:

> *Living together with Adam at L'Arche Daybreak has profoundly influenced my prayer, my sense of myself, my spirituality, and my ministry. Adam, the man who suffers from severe epilepsy, and whose life has seemingly been limited because of his many disabilities, has touched the lives of hundreds of L'Arche assistants, visitors, and friends.*

Henri was delayed at Canadian immigration, but finally joined Adam's parents and other Daybreak friends around Adam's hospital bed. Longing to connect with Adam's body, *I kissed him on the forehead and stroked his hair.* Those gathered prayed with Adam, then *after that we just sat with him, following his breathing.*

Adam died peacefully that night. On February 14, 1996, Henri went to the funeral home. *Seeing Adam's body in the casket touched me deeply. He looked so peaceful, like a young man who had just fallen asleep. Tears filled my eyes. I couldn't stop looking at him.*

In his reflections at Adam's funeral, Henri identified how Adam's gentle physical presence had affected everyone who knew him. It was a true story about the body. Henri summed it up later:

> *Adam gave me a sense of belonging. He rooted me in the truth of my physical being, anchored me in my community, and gave me a deep experience of God's presence in our life together. Without having touched Adam, I don't know where I would be today. Those first fourteen months at Daybreak, washing, feeding, and just sitting with Adam, gave me the home I had been yearning for; not just a home with good people but a home in my own body, in the body of my community, in the body of the church, yes, in the body of God. I had heard and read about the life of Jesus, but I was never able to touch or see him. I was able to touch Adam. Each of us who has touched Adam has been made whole somewhere; it has been our common experience.*

A FEW WEEKS AFTER Adam's death, Henri and his friend Frank Hamilton traveled to New Mexico. *"When you go to Santa Fe, be sure to visit my friend Jim,"* Fred Rogers urged them. Jim Smith, a writer and publisher, suggested lunch at his favorite El Dorado Hotel. They enjoyed a leisurely lunch *speaking about our personal histories, spirituality, books, and, of course, Santa Fe.* Delighted with their new acquaintance, Henri and Frank invited him for dinner a few nights later.

It became a quite remarkable evening. After dinner I showed him the video "Angels over the Net" about the Flying Rodleighs, and told him that I always wanted to write a book about them but hadn't found the right form.

Jim responded quite radically: "You must write the book because you have given it so much of your energy and attention. You have to trust your intuition that your friendship with these trapeze artists allows you to say something very important about the meaning of life."

I said: "Yes indeed, that intuition is deep and strong, but I am afraid. When I first saw the Rodleighs, something very deep and intimate within me was touched. They brought back in a very vivid way the longings I had as a seventeen-year old boy for communion, community, and intimacy.

"Much of the longings went underground during my time at the seminary and the university and my many years of teaching. They only manifested themselves in occasional mental wanderings, curiosities, and feelings of anguish. When I went to L'Arche I allowed all these feelings and emotions and passions to reemerge.

"But seeing the Rodleighs catapulted me in a new consciousness. There in the air I saw the artistic realization of my deepest yearnings. It was so intense that even today I do not dare to write about it because it requires a radical new step not only in my writing but also in my life."

Jim said: "I knew all this. The video showed it to me. The Rodleighs are completing something within you that for many years remained uncompleted. It has to do with your sexuality, your search for community, and your deep yearning for completeness. When you do not write the book you will deny yourself an enormous opportunity for growth."

Jim's directness and his challenge amazed Henri. "But what is the book finally about?" he asked.

Jim answered: "About community in the most universal sense. It is the longing of all people that you can express through the Rodleighs' story. It is not just about flying and catching, but about that invisible community that undergirds all that you are seeing in the Rodleighs. You see friendship, family, cooperation, artistic expression, love and commitment, and much more. And that's your final subject."

35

In May 1996, Henri returned to Santa Fe to spend a week writing with Jim's mentorship.

> *What I most hope is to learn how to write a good story that en-*
> *gages the reader to the very end. I realize that Jesus told stories and*
> *that most spiritual masters told stories. I am busy writing about*
> *Adam and plan to write about the Flying Rodleighs. I know what I*
> *want said, but I do not know how to say it.*

Henri arrived in Santa Fe on May 19, 1996, in time for another lunch together.

> *Although I had come to Santa Fe to ask for Jim's help in my writ-*
> *ing, our first conversation was focused on what to do with your life*
> *between 60 and 80!*
>
> *For me this is an increasing important and anxiety-provoking*
> *question. Over the years I have built up a certain reputation. People*

think of me as a Catholic priest, spiritual writer, member of a community with mentally handicapped people, a lover of God, and a lover of people. It is wonderful to have such a reputation.

But lately I have been experiencing it more and more as restricting, because I feel a certain pressure within me to keep living up to that reputation and to do, say, and write things that fit the expectations of those who know me. The Catholic Church, L'Arche, my family, my friends, my readers etc. all have an agenda they want me to follow.

But since I am in my sixties, new thoughts, feelings, emotions, and passions have arisen within me that are not all in line with my previous thoughts, feelings, emotions, and passions.

What is my responsibility to the world around me and what is my responsibility to myself? What does it mean to be faithful to my vocation? Does it require to be consistent with my earlier way of living and thinking or does it ask for the courage to move in new directions even when that will disappoint many?

I am more and more aware that Jesus died when he was in his early thirties. I have already lived more than thirty years longer than Jesus. How would Jesus have lived and thought when he had lived that long? I don't know.

But for me new questions and concerns emerge at my present age that weren't there in the past. They refer to all the levels of life: intimacy, community, prayer, friendship, work, church, God, life, and death.

How can I be free enough not to be afraid of these questions, and to let them emerge whatever the consequences? It feels quite frightening.

IN THE MIDDLE OF the week, Joan Kroc's plane picked up Henri for lunch in San Diego. They had both been reading biographies of artists: Joan was reading about the poet Gerard Manley Hopkins, and Henri had just finished reading an account of painter Georgia O'Keeffe's life. Joan warmly thanked Henri for the boxes of O'Keeffe art cards that he brought her.

> *The more I read about O'Keeffe and look at her paintings, I feel a deep affinity to her. Her struggles in relationships and her struggle to develop her own artform—going back and forth between New York and New Mexico—reveal a person with great needs for love, affection, and personal support but also for independence, freedom, solitude, and space for creativity. Her intense search for intimacy and solitude are part of the art she created.*

After lunch, Joan treated them both to dishes of ice cream. *Driving home, Joan balanced her ice cream cup on the steering wheel with the result that we were zigzagging on the road. I kept shouting, "Be careful—you nearly hit that curve—look out—oh you got real close to that car—" She said, "Oh how funny, you are scared."* But she conceded that they could pull off the road to eat their ice cream.

Henri returned to his writing in New Mexico. He pondered his conversations with Jim about his fears, questions, and longings as he looked ahead in his life. At the end of the week, he carefully gathered up piles of notes and his manuscript, slipping the thick files into his worn leather briefcase. He had been inspired by stimulating time with artistic personalities. He had even drafted most of a book. But it was a book about his friend Adam. He still had written nothing more about the Flying Rodleighs.

36

The hydraulic lift moves, a whirring sound with a slight whine. Henri finds the sound curiously soothing. He is glad that Dennie is with him. He prefers not to travel alone.

·····

EARLY IN JULY, HENRI jumped off the train in Oberursel, Germany, and looked around eagerly for Rodleigh. They greeted each other with a big hug and hurried back to the circus.

July 9, 1996

I hadn't expected that I would be so moved seeing the Rodleighs again. But I found myself crying as I saw them flying and catching under the circus cupola.

As I watched them in the air I felt some of the same profound emotions that I felt when I saw them for the first time with my father in 1991. It is the emotion hard to describe but it is the emotion coming from the experience of an enfleshed spirituality. Body and spirit are fully united. The body in its beauty and elegance expresses the spirit of love, friendship, family, and community and the spirit never leaves the here and now of the body.

Rodleigh watched Henri. "I wish that I could put Henri into my body to experience the exhilaration of flight to the catcher and our celebration when we return safely," he lamented to Jennie. He really wanted Henri to have the experience of rising, the momentum of leaving the fly bar and going upward, rising into the trick, then being caught by the catcher swinging up from underneath. There was no way Henri's body could do anything like that, but even a limited experience would be better than nothing, Rodleigh figured. The next day, he suggested to Jon that at least they could give Henri a hint of their experience, and so Henri once more tried the trapeze, this time with a catcher.

At the end of the practice session Rodleigh asked me if I would like to make a swing or two. First he helped me to get into the net and showed me how to climb the long ladder to the pedestal. It was my second time since getting to know the Rodleighs that I stood on the pedestal. It is an intimidating place to be. The space below above and around me felt enormously large and awesome. Kerri and Slava put the safety belt around me, held me tight, and handed me the bar. As I held the bar I wondered if I would be able to hold my own weight, but as they lifted me off I felt at ease swinging above the net a few times. I tried to kick a little to get higher but simply didn't have much breath left, so Rodleigh said "hop" and let me drop myself into the net. I repeated the whole sequence once more, with a tiny bit more grace.

Then Rodleigh wanted me to have a sense of the catcher's grip. So

I climbed the ladder at the catcher's side and Jon, who was hanging head down on the catch bar, grabbed me by the wrists and held me hanging there for a while. I looked up at his upside-down face and could imagine how it would be to swing while held by him. Altogether I was happy with the experience. It got me as close as I will ever come to being a trapeze artist!

After the afternoon show Rodleigh invited me to join him in the truck as he put new bandages on the trapeze bar. I didn't know how much care is needed to do this. Practically every week new gauze has to be tightly wrapped around the bar, so that it doesn't move when the flyer grabs it and very even so that it does not cause blisters on the flyers' hands.

Jennie has made a video of the practice session and of the afternoon show. Seeing myself hanging on the trapeze bar made me feel silly. It was a pathetic sight.

But seeing the whole afternoon act in slow motion was a great treat. More than anything else, a slow-motion presentation of the complicated tricks makes you appreciate the highly skillful art of the Rodleighs.

During the evening show I realized how anxious I am when I watch the Rodleighs at work. The more I know about their act, the harder it is to watch it. Knowing the Rodleighs so well and being aware of how much can go wrong, I look at them as a mother who sees her children doing dangerous things. I felt great relief when everything came to a good end. The large audience was ecstatic, stamping their feet and clapping their hands with wild enthusiasm.

At the end of Henri's visit, Rodleigh and Jennie drove him to the Frankfurt rail station. *It was a warm and heartfelt good-bye. I realize how much our friendship has grown over the years and how much we have come to enjoy each other's presence. The two days in Oberursel were very life giving for me and I realize how being with the Rodleighs is one of the best ways for me to really "be away from it all" and to experience relaxation and restoration.*

37

Dennie sighs as he looks down at the parking lot. He is not surprised to see that a small crowd has assembled, attracted by the well-equipped emergency trucks, intrigued by the sight of someone flying out the window. The day is cloudy, a little cool. Probably even more people will be watching from the hotel windows. He can't blame them. It is an unusual sight. It is hard to protect a patient's privacy: you really can't keep a window rescue hidden. Henri's eyes are closed. Dennie hopes that Henri won't feel too exposed when he becomes aware of the spectators.

"I can see our ambulance driver and the other firefighters waiting on the ground for us," Dennie says to Henri. Then he adds somewhat apologetically, "So much unusual activity has drawn an audience. I am afraid it is a bit of a circus."

Henri seems to smile slightly, but he does not answer.

·····•

A FEW DAYS AFTER seeing the Flying Rodleighs, Henri pulled out the final journals he had acquired for his sabbatical, their hard covers featuring art from New York's Metropolitan Museum of Art. These last two journals were identical, with glowing golden covers showing details of the four-thousand-year-old Egyptian sarcophagus of Khnumnakht. Henri studied a journal cover with its painted door between the lands of the living and the dead. Large, pensive eyes painted above the doorway looked from the land of eternity to the land of the living, greeting him each day as he continued his record of his sabbatical year. They reminded him of something he had written in 1992: *I know now that I have to speak from eternity into time, from lasting joy into the passing realities of our short existence in this world. One could call it the "prophetic vision": looking at people and this world through the eyes of God.*

THE RELAXED DAYS WITH Rodleigh and the troupe had been a welcome respite. The spring and summer of 1996 were stressful.

His mind often returned to the questions raised in his conversations with Jim Smith in Santa Fe about how to live the next decades of his life. For years, some friends had urged him to come out as a gay man and be a role model. Aware that his sexual orientation could be revealed without his consent, Henri was often uneasy. By July, he was writing about his *unresolvable struggle* to a friend: *My sexuality will remain a great source of suffering to me until I die. I don't think there is any "solution." The pain is truly "mine" and I have to own it. Any "relational solution" will be a disaster. I feel deeply called by God to live my vows well even when it means a lot of pain. But I trust that the pain will be fruitful.*

On July 31, 1996, Henri sat down and opened his journal. He had confided in his friend Nathan Ball. *I finally felt ready to talk with Nathan about the anxiety that had been plaguing me during the last few months. I felt somewhat embarrassed and ashamed to put my inner burden on my best friend, but I am very glad I did. Nathan felt it hard not so much to listen to my pain but to realize that I had walked with it so long without sharing it with him.*

As he read what he had written, he automatically began to gnaw on his fingernails, then stared at them, surprised to find they were already so well chewed. *I often wonder how I would survive emotionally without his faithful friendship,* he added.

THE NEXT WEEKS OF Henri's sabbatical were full, but the trapeze book was never far from his mind. *Trapeze was my secret door,* he had written earlier that spring to Jim Smith. *But I felt I could not be able to walk through it alone. The trapeze is the place to walk together.* Jim read that several times before writing back. Calling the trapeze a door to walk through together should have been a confusing metaphor, but he liked it. It was an invitation.

38

In August, Joan Kroc invited Henri to visit her in California for the weekend to continue their conversations about the spiritual life. Her jet would again pick him up.

She welcomed me warmly and took me right away to a restaurant. Four of Joan's friends from New York were waiting. Knowing Henri's interest in art, Joan had invited the art consultant who had helped build her art collection. *A very kind and gentle man. But now he is the victim of Alzheimer's disease and needs constant nursing care. A young man who has been his nurse for the past eight months was with him at the table. During the lunch, he was remarkably alert and we were able to have a good conversation.*

Henri enjoyed discussing art, religion, and spirituality over lunch. He and Joan carried on around Lake Hodges, stopping for a drink at a little Mexican restaurant. When they returned to Joan's, Henri settled happily into an afternoon nap before the two of them went out for dinner at Mille Fleurs restaurant.

Over dinner, we talked quite seriously about abortion and the right to life issues. I told her much about Adam. Without Adam, my own life and the lives of many others would not have been so richly blessed.

The next morning, Joan drove Henri in her Jaguar convertible to pick up breakfast: croissants with ham from Burger King. *"This is a special treat. I know I am a naughty girl,"* the heir to the McDonald's fortune told Henri.

Sitting on Joan's terrace, I explained to Joan God's desire to come always closer to us. God is the God-for-us, who protects us, the God-with-us who shares our human struggles, and the God-within-us who dwells in our heart. Three ways of God relating to us in faithfulness.

God does not want to be feared. God wants to be loved. God wants to be as close to us as we are to ourselves, closer even. Joan listened with great attention and we had a very good conversation, quite personal, quite honest, quite sincere.

By lunchtime, Joan decided Henri needed to play.

"Let's go to the races in Del Mar," Joan said. *"I have my own box there and we can have a nice lunch while doing a little betting. After your lesson in spirituality, I will give you a lesson in decadence!"*

It was quite an experience! We sat in a box, which was a lovely lounge with betting machines and a large balcony overlooking the racetrack with a TV to give you close-ups of the races. Joan gave me a voucher for fifty dollars to play with. Soon I wanted to win! I quickly experienced the power of gambling. "Maybe next time I will make a fortune, maybe next time, maybe next time."

Finally, Joan suggested it was time to go. *When we left, I had lost more than won. Joan said, "Why don't you cash your voucher, so you have the feeling you won something?" I cashed the voucher and got thirty-two dollars.*

When we got home again, we celebrated the liturgy in the living room. Joan said, "Why don't we ask Angela, our cook, to join us?" It was Saturday afternoon, but Henri would spend most of Sunday flying back to New Jersey, so he used the Bible readings for the Sunday Mass. "Let the peoples praise you, O God; let all the peoples praise you," they said together at the Psalm.

Joan watched Henri raise his large hands as he had thousands of times in the priestly gesture that he loved so much, lifting the body of Christ in the consecrated bread.

Later, over dinner, Joan had something on her mind. "Henri," she said, then paused. Usually it was Henri who had new insights into God. "You know what you were saying about God, for us, with us, within us? Have you ever thought that when you say Mass and lift the bread and say 'the Body of Christ,' it is like the trapeze act you're always talking about? It's as if Jesus flies to you, and you are the catcher."

Henri stared at Joan, then at his hands, astonished. He had never thought of this. He had written often about his aging hands, about how he stretched out his hands to bless people. But now he imagined that his hands reached for God who is already in motion, catching and holding the body of Jesus in that moment of consecration. Cradling. For almost forty years, he had been catching God.

Joan grinned at his wide eyes. "You know how you are always telling me to trust, trust, trust? Maybe God also has to trust. To trust you. To trust all of us."

She poured Henri another glass of the 1973 Rothschild wine she had opened to drink together. Henri sipped it, savoring both the velvety wine and this new insight.

Joan pressed forward. "Remember that letter you sent to me last year? I remember almost every word. You wrote, *'strange as it may sound, we can become like God for others. It becomes possible to love without demanding love in return. It is a strong, energetic, vital, and very active love.'* The love you described is disciplined, even athletic, like a trapeze artist."

She and Henri had often shared about how hard they found it to believe in God's unconditional love and to trust themselves. "That love sends us out to serve joyously, like you keep saying," Joan added. "If God trusts us, then we can trust ourselves."

39

Lying on the stretcher, Henri concentrates on breathing slowly, the way Dennie had taught him. In, two, three, and out, two, three. In, two, three, and out, two, three.

In, two, three, and out, two, three.

Life is a precarious balance. Sometimes I'm out of balance and then writing helps me find it again. I just want to write down the things that occupy my mind so in the end I know more about my own struggle.

Out of balance. Earlier in the spring, he had confessed in his journal, *I feel quite anxious interiorly. I feel quite powerless in the face of these free-floating emotions of love, hate, rejection, attraction, gratitude, and regret. I realize that I am walking around with some deep, covered-up emotions and that not much is needed to bring that to the surface and throw me off balance.*

Henri takes another breath, then lets it out with a sigh. Off balance indeed. Maybe those disturbing covered-up emotions reveal that his life has been one off-balance failure after another. He tries poking at some of his familiar insecurities, like prodding a sore tooth to see if it still hurts.

What about the book he keeps promising the Rodleighs? They are skilled, magnificent artists. They are bound to be disappointed in whatever he writes.

He tries another question, testing to see how tender it feels: Has his entire life been a pointless story of drifting from place to place like a hungry ghost? Does it look as pathetic as his efforts on the trapeze? He could imagine his life that way. It is like seeing himself in the video, hanging limply before falling.

But strapped onto his stretcher now, his long-running fears are getting no traction. In fact, they seem almost comical. Henri remembers how his embarrassment over the sight of himself haplessly clutching the trapeze quickly turned to amusement in the presence of his cheerful friends. They had chuckled watching the video, and when Henri complained that the video showed that he had two left feet and only thumbs on his hands, their affectionate laughter increased.

In their amusement was unconditional acceptance. As they chortled, Henri could not help laughing, too, joining in the mirth even at his own expense. Rodleigh and Jennie and the others did not judge his effort as sad. They loved offering him that trapeze experience, and they were proud of him for eagerly grasping the opportunity.

Also, he thinks, the sorry sight of his skinny body dangling from the trapeze was the view from the outside. His inner experience was dynamic! He did it. He climbed the swinging rope ladder. With the support of the troupe members, he reached out for the fly bar and launched off the pedestal. Even Rodleigh had been impressed by his eager fearlessness. Hanging for a few moments holding the catcher's hands, looking at Jon's upside-down smiling face was thrilling. Even letting go entirely and dropping into the bouncy net was a joyful experience because it was shared with friends.

No, pathetic would have been refusing that overwhelming physical desire to go to Selma, and missing the experience of offering a ride to Charles, then walking, singing, eating, and sleeping with fear and joy in that extraordinary community. Or staying in his mainly White enclave of people rather than going to be with Martin Luther King Jr.'s people at his funeral. Pathetic would have been staying at Harvard, getting more miserable and lonely by the day. It would have been pathetic to reject the invitation to join the Daybreak community, or to shy away from surprising friendships with Bill, Adam, and so many others. Or to give in to his fear of rejection and not return to Daybreak after his emotional break. Or be too afraid to go to the National Catholic HIV/AIDS Ministry conferences.

And truly pathetic would have been to stay seated in the bleachers at the circus, aching to meet the artists but immobilized by his own self-consciousness.

Instead, he followed his heart, his inner call, even when it meant giving up security, reaching out over and over for something not yet within his grasp.

Of course he has often felt off-balance, he realizes. A flyer needs to lose their balance entirely, reaching out from the platform for the trapeze and committing their body to the forward movement before the trapeze is fully in their grasp. Losing balance is the only way to do it.

It's been a life of trust. And it's not over yet. He can't wait to tell Rodleigh that he flew out a window.

Even with all the monitors on his chest, he feels less anxious than he has in a long time, full of compassion for his fearful, vulnerable self, fumbling to choose a generous life with courage. Many times in his life he has fallen, often not very gracefully.

Just months ago, he had encouraged Joan Kroc: *When we radically claim God's unconditional love for us, we can forgive those who have wounded us and set them free by our forgiveness.* From his aerial act on his stretcher, Henri thinks of the Flying Rodleighs' frank discussion after each performance of their successes and failures together. He sends out a small prayer of contrition and goodwill, forgiving everyone, forgiving himself.

Living means there will be falls. It's life, all of life. How often has he told other people that?

> *I sometimes have thought, how would it be if I had no desire anymore to judge anyone? I would walk on the earth as a very light person.*

Henri glimpses what it would be like also to stop judging himself, to see even his own life *through the eyes of God.* Trapeze artists can't perform by themselves. *A trick is not complete unless it is done from the board, successfully caught by the catcher, and then successfully returned to pedestal board.* Flyers need to trust their catcher not just to safely gather them in, he remembers, but to relaunch them into further flying.

> *The Rodleighs are saying to me indirectly, don't be afraid to fly a little, don't be afraid to take a few doubles or triples or a few layouts. If you really miss the catcher you fall into the net, so what's the big issue? After all, take a risk and trust, trust, trust. That's how it ap-*

plies to my life. You know life is full of new possibilities, full of new adventures, and I just want to keep trying out what life is all about.

He feels lighter and lighter.

THE LIFT REACHES THE bottom with a jolt.

Dennie's voice: "We are here. You don't have to do anything. There are eight firemen to move you into the ambulance!"

Henri opens his eyes, momentarily confused, surprised to find he has fully descended.

He feels like he has been rising.

EPILOGUE

As the three flyers swung away from the pedestal board, they somersaulted and turned freely in the air, only to be safely grasped by their two catchers. I somehow caught a glimpse of the mystery of being the Beloved: the mystery in which complete freedom and complete bonding are one and in which letting go of everything and being connected with everything no longer elude each other.

Henri didn't die. At least, not then. Within minutes, he arrived safely at the hospital.

Henri's father came with his brothers and sister to be with him. Across an ocean, Henri's Daybreak community gathered to pray for him, and put his friend Nathan on an overnight flight to arrive Tuesday morning.

Henri said to Nathan, "I don't think I'm going to die, but if I do please tell everyone that I am grateful. I am so very grateful."

By Thursday morning, the danger had passed and Henri made plans to come home. There was minimal heart damage. At Daybreak, we relaxed and started to joke, "When God closes a door, God opens a window."

On Friday, Henri prayed evening prayer with his friends Jan and Nathan, then walked with them to the front doors of the hospital and waved them off.

Early in the morning of Saturday, September 21, still in the hospital, Henri had a massive heart attack and died.

Henri's family came immediately. After praying beside Henri, his father announced that Henri should be buried with the L'Arche community that he had chosen. All his family would accompany his body to Canada after a funeral in Utrecht.

News of Henri's death reached the Flying Rodleighs after their last show that evening. They had expected to see him after his trip to Russia. They sat for a long time quietly remembering their friend, and the next morning their grief weighed down their practice. But at their afternoon show, after they bounded into the ring swirling their sparkling capes, Rodleigh made a short speech dedicating that performance to the memory of their friend Henri, and they performed flawlessly in his honor. During their final bow, Rodleigh looked at the seat where Henri had last sat watching them, wishing the person sitting there was Henri.

At the funeral in the Netherlands four days later, Rodleigh and Jennie again had the experience of being welcomed like old friends by people they had never met. They already knew Henri's family, and Rodleigh was moved when Henri's brother Laurent insisted that Rodleigh replace him as a pallbearer. "Once again I'm supporting Henri's weight in my hands, but this time not on the other end of a safety harness," thought Rodleigh. He and Jennie sat weeping through the funeral service, and Rodleigh fought back his urge to leap up to tell the assembled mourners their experience of a different Henri: relaxed, curious, a little flamboyant, attentive, hilarious, and fun.

Thus there were two funerals: the one in Utrecht that Rodleigh and Jennie Stevens attended, and then another in Canada that gathered more than a thousand people.

Henri's body flew across the ocean in a beautiful classic coffin of natural honey oak. By the time Henri's body arrived in Canada, there were also two caskets. Years earlier, Henri had told the L'Arche Daybreak woodworking program that he wanted us to make him a casket when he died. During the long week as we waited for Henri's return with his family, I invited community members to draw and paint their feelings. Artwork flooded in, full of life and color, and I used it to create a colorful hand-painted lid. Painted in a radiant rainbow, our work of collaborative art looked like a door. At the funeral home near Daybreak, we moved Henri's body into our homemade rectangular pine casket. His brother Laurent and I gently tugged off his necktie to mark that he had finished traveling, and brought him home to Daybreak.

But he wasn't entirely finished with his travels. Henri's body was buried twice. He had wanted to be buried with other members of his Daybreak community, but fourteen years after Henri was buried in a small Roman Catholic cemetery it became apparent that there would be no space available near him for other Daybreak community members.

His friend Bill Van Buren died in 2009 and was buried at St. John's Anglican cemetery, just north of L'Arche Daybreak. Founded in the mid-1800s, this simple historic cemetery had space for many Daybreak members.

So in 2010, at the request of his brother Laurent, Henri's body made one more journey. A specialized backhoe carefully scooped up all that remained of his body, lifting it through the air then settling it into yet another casket.

Henri's body is buried next to Bill's. Gradually, nearly a dozen other members of the L'Arche Daybreak community have joined them. Even in death, their bodies continue to tell a spiritual story, of the mystery of letting go of everything and being connected with everything.

> *I suddenly realized that's what life is all about. We are invited to make a lot of triples and jumps but the great thing is to trust the catcher and to know we will be caught when we come down from our special tricks. Do I dare to let go and to say that will happen even when I am a little scared sometimes? I'm grateful that we could be together—let's pray for one another that what we do in the coming years will be full of courage, full of confidence, and full of trust.*

ACKNOWLEDGMENTS

Henri was fascinated by the Flying Rodleighs' commitment to each other. Trapeze is not an individual art. Each artist has to expect the best of each other, be swift to forgive, have confidence in themselves, and give each other full support to try again. Every performance is new. This spoke to Henri of the artistry of community. It also speaks to the experience of writing a book! Neither Henri nor I ever wrote a book as an individual endeavor. Writing may be solitary, but creating a book is a communal project.

First, of course, my thanks to Henri Nouwen himself, who was a dear friend to me and my family as well as my fellow member of L'Arche Daybreak. It's been twenty-five years since his sudden death, and his energy and spirit live on.

Enormous thanks to my beloved spouse, Geoff Whitney-Brown, without whom this book would have been less nuanced and the process of writing it much less fun. We spent weeks together in the Nouwen Archives at the University of St. Michael's College's Special Collections in Toronto, where Simon Rogers and Liesl Joson were helpful and patient with our barrage of questions and requests.

Huge thanks to Rodleigh Stevens for letting me use his many vivid memories of Henri during those five years when their lives intersected. I eagerly look forward to Rodleigh's memoir of his own remarkable life.

In those early stages, I confided in my friend Ruth Rakoff that Henri's life was stranger than fiction. Ruth pointed out that key to the story is Henri's relationship with his own body, as well as his attraction to many different communities that are often overlooked or marginalized. Frame the story with Henri looking back during his last and most dramatic flight, out the Hilversum window, she suggested. Thank you, Ruth, for giving this book a shape.

How can a patient in the midst of a heart attack be taken out a window? My thanks to Dennie Wulterkens, emergency medical rescue specialist in the Netherlands. Because of Dennie's careful explanations, all details of Henri's Hilversum rescue are portrayed as accurately as possible, based on the norms and protocols of 1996.

Some gratitude spans many years: my tender thanks and love to Laurent Nouwen and his family for their hospitality, ongoing encouragement, and decades of friendship. My affectionate thanks also to Franz and Reny Johna, and to Robert Jonas.

My special appreciation and respect to Henri's close friends who generously offered their encouragement, wisdom, and good-humored insights, especially Patricia Beall Gavigan and Bart Gavigan, Frank Hamilton, Michael Harank, Peter and Anke Naus, Kathy Bruner, Carl McMillan, and Ron P. van den Bosch. Particular thanks to Robert Morgan for permission to quote his speech at Henri's sixtieth birthday.

I am blessed to have friends and family who read various drafts along the way: David Walsh, Celia McLean, Margaret Ford, Monica

Whitney-Brown, Zachary Brabazon, Jordan Lambeth, Barbara Whitney, Jim Loney, Flavia Silano, Janine Langan, Joanne Hincks, Mary Lou Halferty, Stephanie and Joe Mancini, Jean Crowder, Michael Hryniuk, Janet Burlacu, David Whitney-Brown, Diane Marshall, Jamie Bennett, Spencer Dunn, and Maggie Enwright.

My heartfelt thanks to all who responded generously to my sudden calls for help or advice, including Kathryn Dean, Diana Cafazzo, Kerry Wilkins, Vicentiu Burlacu, Rachel Anderson, Dave and Maureen Carter-Whitney, Joe and Donna Abbey-Colborne, Jonathan Heyman, Mike Blair, Victoria MacKay, Jean Chong, Robert Ellsberg, Michael Higgins, Ian Gwynne-Robson, Joe Mihevc, Rosalee Bender, and all the fabulous staff at Munro's Books in Victoria, BC.

Through the years of writing this book, I have appreciated and benefited from my colleagues at the Centre for Studies in Religion and Society at University of Victoria, British Columbia, and at St. Jerome's University, Waterloo, Ontario.

Like a trapeze performance, a book flies out into the world because of a huge unseen community and team. I thank Sue Mosteller and everyone at the Henri Nouwen Legacy Trust for initiating this project and giving me freedom with Henri's trapeze material, trusting I would "catch" it. Warm thanks especially to Karen Pascal, Gabrielle Earnshaw, Judith Leckie, Sally Keefe Cohen, Stephen Lazarus, and Sean Mulrooney. Thanks also to the Canadian Writers Union, and to Warren Sheffer, the most kindhearted and clear-eyed contract lawyer that any writer could want.

Katy Hamilton at HarperOne has been a supportive and enthusiastic editor from the first time she read my manuscript. Chantal Tom and Mickey Maudlin carried the project forward with friendly competence and commitment. My gratitude also to publisher Judith Curr, and to this book's production, publicity, and marketing experts—in other words, everyone on the great team at HarperOne who helped launch this book into flight.

Finally, I want to acknowledge you, our readers. In many ways, Henri's story is about finding the freedom of flying, falling, and catching with others. Whether in L'Arche or Selma or at Martin Luther King Jr.'s funeral or with people gathered by the AIDS pandemic or in friendship with traveling trapeze artists, Henri's story reveals why it is energizing and spiritually renewing to carry our burdens in companionship and solidarity.

Every time Henri talked about the Flying Rodleighs, his eyes would shine and his face would break into a beaming smile. Just remembering filled his whole body with joy. He was eager to share this experience, hoping it would bring readers to a place of *total absorption, total delight.* We live in times when it is easy to feel discouraged or alone, times when it is more important than ever to reach out to connect with others. May Henri's unlikely story help you to find joy, freedom, and beauty in each of your irreplaceable, imperfect communities.

NOTES

Epigraph

vii **"When I saw the Flying Rodleighs":** Henri Nouwen, interview in English in the unedited footage for the film *Angels Over the Net*, produced by Jan van den Bosch (Hilversum: The Company Media Produkties, 1995). A DVD copy of this unedited footage is held in the Nouwen Archives.

vii **"The ten minutes that followed":** Henri J. M. Nouwen, "Chapter I," 9–10. This unpublished draft typed manuscript is held in the Nouwen Archives.

Prologue

1 **When they received the phone call:** Rodleigh Stevens's accounts of hearing about Henri's death, dedicating their performance to Henri, and attending Henri's funeral are found in his unpublished memoir, "What a Friend We Had in Henri," 1. This memoir is held in the Nouwen Archives.

2 **one speaker described Henri as "anguished" and "wounded":** Many biographies also highlight this side of Henri, with titles like *Wounded Prophet* (Michael Ford), *Genius Born of Anguish* (Michael Higgins and Kevin Burns), and *Lonely Mystic* (Michael Ford).

2 **Henri believed his most important book:** Henri's friends Bart and Patricia Gavigan recall a conversation with Henri: "He wanted the circus story to make the cross-over to a secular audience in a way he had never before attempted. He felt it was the most important thing he would ever

write." Bart Gavigan and Patricia Gavigan, "Collision and Paradox," in *Befriending Life: Encounters with Henri Nouwen*, ed. Beth Porter (New York: Doubleday, 2001), 55–56. This conversation with the Gavigans is included in Chapter 14 of this book.

3 **I lived at L'Arche Daybreak . . . where Henri was also a community member:** See www.larche.org: "L'Arche is a worldwide federation of people, with and without intellectual disabilities, working together for a world where all belong. In L'Arche, each person participates, helps and receives help. L'Arche is founded on mutual relationships." Henri spent 1985–86 in a L'Arche community in France, then in 1986 he moved to L'Arche Daybreak in Richmond Hill, Ontario, Canada.

3 **I wrote an introduction to a new edition:** See "Introduction," Memorial Edition of Henri Nouwen's *The Road to Daybreak* (London: DLT, 1997), reprinted in 2013 edition; "Introduction," *A Spirituality of Homecoming*, Henri J. M. Nouwen (Nashville: Upper Room Books, 2012); "How Not to Comfort a New Orleans Hurricane Survivor," in *Turning the Wheel: Henri Nouwen and Our Search for God*, ed. Jonathan Bengtson and Gabrielle Earnshaw (Ottawa: Novalis, 2007), 135–44; "Henri at Daybreak: Celebration and Hard Work," in *Remembering Henri: The Life and Legacy of Henri Nouwen*, ed. Gerald S. Twomey and Claude Pomerleau (Maryknoll, NY: Orbis Books, 2006), 119–37; "Safe in God's Heart," *Sojourners Magazine* 25, no. 6 (November–December 1996); "Lives Lived—Henri J. M. Nouwen," *Globe and Mail*, October 2, 1996.

4 **My main artistic license:** There is some justification for this fictional framing. In his 1990 book *Beyond the Mirror*, Henri claimed he was able to reflect and think even while he was in a painful medical emergency. See Henri J. M. Nouwen, *Beyond the Mirror: Reflections on Death and Life* (New York: Crossroad, 1990), 23–24, 39. He wrote in his 1993 "Circus Diary–Part I" that in times of crisis life can go into a slow-motion experience of heightened awareness, and *"Some people even say they saw their whole life pass by in a second"*—see his Saturday, May 10, entry in Nouwen, "Circus Diary–Part I: Finding the Trapeze Artist in the Priest," *New Oxford Review* 60, no. 5 (June 1993), quoted in Chapter 17. Further, the droperidol and fentanyl medications that Henri was likely given at Hotel Lapershoek by paramedics would have reduced his pain and anxiety, and could have also made him feel chatty or even garrulous. But with an oxygen mask covering his mouth, he

would have been unable to share his thoughts, so I present Henri chatting internally within himself.

5 **"I wasn't thinking of using the Rodleighs as illustrations"**: Sunday, May 17, 1992, entry in "Circus Diary–Part II: Finding a New Way to Get a Glimpse of God," *New Oxford Review* 60, no. 6 (July–August 1993): 10.

Chapter 1

9 **Two paramedics in crisp white uniforms:** Specific details about the paramedics' actions are based upon extensive consultation with Dutch ambulance nurse and emergency medical rescue specialist Dennie Wulterkens.

9 Henri's arrival in Hilversum and call for medical help are described in Michael Ford, *Wounded Prophet: A Portrait of Henri J. M. Nouwen* (New York: Doubleday, 1999), 201; Michael Ford, *Lonely Mystic: A New Portrait of Henri J. M. Nouwen* (New York: Paulist Press, 2018), 143–46. See also Michael O'Laughlin, *Henri Nouwen: His Life and Vision* (Maryknoll, NY: Orbis Books, 2005), 162; and Jurjen Beumer, *Henri Nouwen: A Restless Seeking for God* (New York: Crossroad, 1997), 173.

11 **First he had tried dictating a tape:** Henri dictated his first impressions onto a cassette tape that was subsequently transcribed by Connie Ellis, his secretary back in Canada, and titled "The Flying Rodleighs–The Circus." This unpublished typed transcript is held in the Nouwen Archives.

11 **"What really got to me"**: Nouwen, "The Flying Rodleighs–The Circus," 1–3, 4.

Chapter 2

15 **"Develop the story scene by scene"**: Theodore A. Rees Cheney, *Writing Creative Non-Fiction: How to Use Fiction Techniques to Make Your Nonfiction More Interesting, Dramatic, and Vivid* (Berkeley, CA: Ten Speed Press, 1991), 33. Henri's own copies of his books about writing are still in the library of the house where he lived at L'Arche Daybreak, with his underlining and marginal notes.

15 **"Visiting the south German city of Freiburg has always been a great pleasure"**: Henri J. M. Nouwen, "Chapter I," 1–3. This begins a second attempt by Henri to write about his initial encounters with the Flying Rodleighs, which he simply titled "Chapter I" and "Chapter II." Both

"Chapter I" (as noted above) and "Chapter II" are unpublished typed manu-
scripts held in the Nouwen Archives. All further quotations from Nouwen
in this chapter are from Nouwen's unpublished manuscript, "Chapter I,"
unless otherwise identified.

16 **"to help myself and others to overcome the deep-seated temptation of self-rejection":** This was a theme in many of Henri's books. He
was especially aware of the unique dangers of self-rejection for gay and
lesbian people, writing a chapter titled "The Self-Availability of the Homosexual," in *Is Gay Good? Ethics, Theology, and Homosexuality*, ed. W. Dwight
Oberholtzer (Philadelphia: Westminster Press, 1971). See Michael Ford's
exploration of that essay in *Lonely Mystic*.

16 **"Nonfiction writers limit themselves":** Cheney, *Writing Creative Nonfiction*, 127.

16 **"However, this time in Freiburg was going to become unique":**
Nouwen, "Chapter I," 4, 6–9.

17 **"A scene reproduces the motion of life; life is motion":** Henri underlined this passage in Cheney, *Writing Creative Nonfiction*, 49.

20 **"The Flying Rodleighs were stunning":** Henri calls the women's
performance costumes "swimsuits" in his dictated text. "The Flying
Rodleighs—The Circus," 5.

20 **Henri had always been attracted to men:** See Ford, *Wounded Prophet*,
73, and Ford, *Lonely Mystic*, 56. Henri was cautious in choosing with whom
to speak about his sexual orientation. While many readers intuited that he
was gay, he never came out. He did not write about his sexuality in any text
considered for publication, but he discussed with his publishers the possibility of addressing it in future writings. See Ford, *Wounded Prophet*, 66–67,
141–44, 191–94; Gabrielle Earnshaw, *Love, Henri: Letters on the Spiritual Life*
(New York: Convergent, 2016), xiv–xv; Ford, *Lonely Mystic*, 56–72.

Chapter 3

24 **Just nine months ago in Prague he wrote in his journal:** Saturday,
January 20, 1996, entry in Henri J. M. Nouwen, original handwritten 1995–
96 sabbatical journals, held in the Nouwen Archives. See also Henri J. M.
Nouwen, *Sabbatical Journey: The Diary of His Final Year* (New York: Crossroad,
1998), 91.

25 **Even back in his university days, Henri's friends saw him as a social climber:** See Carolyn Whitney-Brown, "Lives Lived: Henri J. M. Nouwen," *Globe and Mail*, October 2, 1996. See also Peter Naus, "A Man of Creative Contradictions," *Befriending Life*, 80–81.

25 **All his life, Henri had wanted a different body:** For a sensitive literary discussion of the complexities of "growing up" as a queer child and adolescent, see Kathryn Bond Stockton, *The Queer Child, or Growing Sideways in the Twentieth Century* (Durham, NC: Duke University Press, 2009). Stockton was one of Henri's students in the 1980s at Yale Divinity School. Interestingly, she names her first experience of kissing a woman as "self-defenestration." *Making Out, Avidly Reads* series (New York: New York University Press, 2019), 15–17.

25 **His mother blamed the strict instructions:** See Ford, *Wounded Prophet*, 72–73. Henri also wrote about Holland's hungry winter of 1944–45 when many people were starving, describing his deep grief as a child when the Nouwen family's hungry gardener stole Walter, Henri's beloved pet goat, to feed his family. Henri J. M. Nouwen, *Here and Now: Living in the Spirit* (New York: Crossroads, 1994), 48–49.

26 **Henri is seized with a desire to tell Dennie more about himself:** Michael Ford writes about Nouwen's "tendency to strike up conversations of great intimacy with strangers" (*Wounded Prophet*, 144; see also 213).

26 **An interviewer in 1995 asked Henri:** Nouwen, interview in English in the unedited footage for the film *Angels Over the Net*.

Chapter 4

27 All Nouwen quotations in this chapter are from Nouwen's unpublished manuscript, "Chapter I," unless otherwise identified.

27 **no one had ever told him that grief felt so much like fear:** This is the first sentence of C. S. Lewis's *A Grief Observed* (first published in 1961). While Henri likely had an earlier edition of Lewis's book, the copy in his library at Daybreak is a 1989 edition. C. S. Lewis, *A Grief Observed* (San Francisco: Harper & Row, 1989), 3.

29 **Karlene was uneasy when the circus owner:** This account draws on Stevens, "What a Friend We Had in Henri," 2.

Chapter 5

32 All Nouwen quotations in this chapter are from Nouwen's unpublished manuscript, "Chapter I," unless otherwise identified.

32 **He has used Ativan for more than seven years:** Henri's use of Ativan and his discussion about it with his doctor, as well as the quotations, come from the unpublished "Thursday March 21, '96" entry in Nouwen, handwritten 1995–96 sabbatical journals.

33 **Writing about shared human experiences:** See Henri J. M. Nouwen, *Our Greatest Gift: A Meditation on Dying and Caring* (New York: HarperCollins, 1994), 4–5.

34 **Rodleigh sighed as he headed backstage:** All details from Rodleigh Stevens's perspective are drawn from Stevens, "What a Friend We Had in Henri," 2–3.

Chapter 6

41 **When Henri had a serious accident in 1988:** Nouwen, *Beyond the Mirror*.

41 **"Everything has changed":** Nouwen, *Beyond the Mirror*, 31.

42 **"as if some strong hand had stopped me":** Nouwen, *Beyond the Mirror*, 31.

42 **"Notwithstanding the severe pain, I had a completely unexpected sense of security":** Nouwen, *Beyond the Mirror*, 39.

42 **"A long time of solitude in a Trappist monastery interrupting a busy life of teaching":** Nouwen, *Beyond the Mirror*, 15–16.

42 **After all:** The Dutch are famously stereotyped as being meticulous and organized. See Henri's description of himself in Nouwen, *Beyond the Mirror*: "Knowing my very impatient disposition and aware of my need to stay in control . . ." (39).

42 **march in Selma that interrupted his studies:** See Chapter 10 notes; Nouwen, "We Shall Overcome: A Pilgrimage to Selma, 1965," in *The Road to Peace: Writings on Peace and Justice*, ed. John Dear (Maryknoll, NY: Orbis Books, 1998), 75–95.

43 **The actual painting is enormous:** For a description of the painting and the chair that Henri was given to view it, see Henri J. M. Nouwen, *The Return of the Prodigal Son: A Meditation on Fathers, Brothers, and Sons* (New York: Doubleday, 1992), 7–10.

5

5555555555555

44 **"I am here to write, not to go to the circus!":** Nouwen, "Chapter I," 25.

44 **"The next morning while sitting at my desk, I kept looking at my watch":** Nouwen, "Chapter II," 1. The following Nouwen quotations and details in this chapter are from Nouwen's unpublished manuscript, "Chapter II," unless otherwise identified.

45 **Rodleigh was eager to work on his new routine that morning:** Stevens, "What a Friend We Had in Henri," 4.

Chapter 7

50 **"Is this trapeze act perhaps one of the windows in the house of life":** Nouwen, "Chapter II," 8–10. All Nouwen quotations in this chapter are from Nouwen's unpublished manuscript, "Chapter II," unless otherwise identified.

51 **The practice ended:** The account in the rest of this chapter except for Henri's words draws on Stevens, "What a Friend We Had in Henri," 4–6.

Chapter 8

54 **"At the very end, they let themselves fall into the net":** Nouwen, "The Flying Rodleighs–The Circus," 29.

55 **"On one channel a rock concert with Tina Turner":** Unpublished March 6, 1986, entry in Nouwen, 1985–86 journals. These unpublished typed transcripts are held in the Nouwen Archives. Henri simplifies the Tina Turner concert to just Turner and David Bowie, but video footage available on YouTube of Tina Turner's 1985 Birmingham performance shows Bryan Adams singing "It's Only Love" with Turner, then Turner and Bowie sing "Tonight" together.

Chapter 9

58 **"For the next few days, I kept going to the circus as often as possible":** Nouwen, "Chapter II," 14–16. All Nouwen quotations in this chapter are from Nouwen's unpublished manuscript, "Chapter II," unless otherwise identified.

59 **Henri wanted to stay backstage:** Stevens, "What a Friend We Had in Henri," 5–6.

Chapter 10

64 **"Sunday was the last day of the Circus Barum in Freiburg":**
Nouwen, "Chapter II," 21–27.

Chapter 11

68 **"It all began with a feeling of restlessness":** This account of Henri's
journey to Selma, participation in the march, and return home to Topeka
draws on Nouwen, "We Shall Overcome," 75–95. All Nouwen quotations
and details in this chapter are from "We Shall Overcome" unless otherwise
identified.

71 **"Resistance that makes for peace"** and **"Individual people, even
the best and strongest":** Henri J. M. Nouwen, *Peacework: Prayer, Resistance, Community* (Maryknoll, NY: Orbis Books, 2005), 97.

71 **that Martin Luther King Jr. was killed:** This account of Henri's participation in Martin Luther King Jr.'s funeral draws on Henri J. M. Nouwen,
"Were You There? The Death of Dr. Martin Luther King Jr., 1968," in *The
Road to Peace,* ed. John Dear, 96–105. The following Nouwen quotations and
details in this chapter about King's funeral are from "Were You There?"
unless otherwise identified.

73 **"You know in this world where there is so much division":** Nouwen,
interview in English in the unedited footage for the film *Angels Over the Net.*

Chapter 12

74 **But just five years earlier:** This account of Henri's move to Daybreak
in the autumn of 1986 draws on Sue Mosteller, "Funeral Eulogy for Henri
Nouwen," in *Seeds of Hope: A Henri Nouwen Reader*, ed. Robert Durback (New
York: Image Books, 1997), 17–18, and Ford, *Wounded Prophet*, 157–58. See
also Mary Bastedo, "Henri and Daybreak: A Story of Mutual Transformation," in *Befriending Life*, 27–29.

75 **Longtime community member Sue Mosteller had welcomed:** It is
impossible to overstate the importance of Sue Mosteller in Henri Nouwen's
life from this point on. See Gabrielle Earnshaw, *Henri Nouwen and the Return
of the Prodigal Son: The Making of a Spiritual Classic* (Orleans, MA: Paraclete
Press, 2020), 67.

75 **His physical experiences of solidarity:** Henri's journal of his time in

Latin America was published as *Gracias! A Latin American Journal* (Maryknoll, NY: Orbis Books, 1983).

76 **"I was told that L'Arche's mission was to 'live with' core members"**: Henri J. M. Nouwen, *Adam, God's Beloved* (Maryknoll, NY: Orbis Books, 1997), 41.

76 **"I live in a house with six handicapped people and four assistants"**: Henri J. M. Nouwen, "Adam's Story: The Peace That Is Not of This World," in Durback, ed., *Seeds of Hope*, 254–55, which was originally a talk given at Harvard St. Paul's Catholic Church, Cambridge, February 10, 1987.

77 **During the past few months I have developed**: Henri J. M. Nouwen, "L'Arche and the World," in *The Road to Peace*, ed. John Dear, 166–67.

78 **"Adam is the weakest person of our family"**: Nouwen, "Adam's Story," 255–56.

79 **"I was aghast"**: Nouwen, *Adam*, 42.

79 **"It takes me about an hour and a half to wake Adam up"**: Nouwen, "Adam's Story," 256.

80 **"I had to get behind him and support him with my body"**: Nouwen, *Adam*, 43, 46.

Chapter 13

82 **"When I think about Circus Barum and Daybreak"**: Wednesday, May 6, diary entry in Nouwen, "Circus Diary–Part I," 9.

83 **why, Henri wonders**: For Henri's account of his breakdown see *Adam*, 78–80, and Henri J. M. Nouwen, *The Inner Voice of Love: A Journey Through Anguish to Freedom* (New York: Doubleday, 1996), xiii–xvii. See also Ford, *Wounded Prophet*, 168–71.

83 **moving from an "issue-oriented life" to a "person-oriented life"**: Henri asserted that this movement was accomplished by joining L'Arche; see Nouwen, "L'Arche and the World," 168.

83 **"I began to realize that the gentle safety of the New House"**: The following quotations are from Nouwen, *Adam*, 78–80, unless otherwise identified.

86 **"When you find yourself curious about the lives of people"**: "22 Feb '88" entry in Henri J. M Nouwen, handwritten 1987–88 journal. The

journal is held in the Nouwen Archives. Selections from this journal were later published in Nouwen, *The Inner Voice of Love*.

86 **"A new spirituality is being born in you":** "22 Feb '88" entry in Nouwen, handwritten 1987–88 journal.

86 **He now lived in the community retreat house:** Carolyn Whitney-Brown's memories of Henri's home in the L'Arche Daybreak community.

Chapter 14

87 **As Rodleigh drove away from Freiburg:** Stevens, "What a Friend We Had in Henri," 6–7.

88 **"After Circus Barum had left Freiburg and I had returned to Toronto":** Nouwen, "Circus Diary—Part I," 8. All further quotations from Nouwen are from "Circus Diary—Part I" unless otherwise identified.

88 **"That was wonderful!" were Henri's delighted first words:** Stevens, "What a Friend We Had in Henri," 7–11.

90 **Back in Canada soon afterward:** This account of Henri's conversation with the Gavigans comes from "Collision and Paradox," *Befriending Life*, 55–56, augmented with their further memories in December 2020.

Chapter 15

95 **"Karlene was making these tapes with her camera":** Nouwen, "The Flying Rodleighs—The Circus," 8–10, 14–15.

97 **In the months after Henri returned:** See Whitney-Brown, "Henri at Daybreak," 122–25.

98 **In January, L'Arche Daybreak threw him:** A video made by the community of Henri's sixtieth birthday party at Daybreak is held in the Nouwen Archives. My account of the party comes from this video and from personal memories.

Chapter 16

101 **"What is the risk?" was a key question:** These quotations are selected from Henri's unpublished handwritten notes during the Gavigan workshop, held in the Nouwen Archives.

Chapter 17

104 **"Back in Toronto, when I spoke about my experience":** Nouwen, "Circus Diary—Part I," 9. All Nouwen quotations in this chapter are from "Circus Diary—Part I" unless otherwise identified. I have made some minor adjustments in Henri's technical description following advice given to me by Rodleigh Stevens.

104 **Rodleigh and the troupe were delighted:** This account of Henri's travels and visit with the Flying Rodleighs in May 1992 draws on Stevens, "What a Friend We Had in Henri," 12–14.

Chapter 18

112 All Nouwen quotations in this chapter are from "Circus Diary—Part I" unless otherwise identified.

113 **After three days, Henri looked like he had been with them for years:** This account of Henri's interactions with the troupe draws on Stevens, "What a Friend We Had in Henri," 14–16.

114 **"What you say is incredibly important for life, not just for the trapeze":** Nouwen, interview in English in the unedited footage for the film *Angels Over the Net*. This quotation is also included in the final English version of the film *Angels Over the Net*.

Chapter 19

117 All Nouwen quotations in this chapter are from "Circus Diary—Part I" unless otherwise identified.

118 **Rodleigh and the troupe knew that their trip would be slower with Henri:** Stevens, "What a Friend We Had in Henri," 16.

122 **"The trip on the German roads from Datteln to Kamen last night":** This and the following Nouwen quotations are from "Circus Diary—Part II."

123 **Jennie glanced at Rodleigh and rolled her eyes:** Based on Stevens, "What a Friend We Had in Henri," 16.

Chapter 20

127 **"The longer I am here, the more I find to write about"**: All Nouwen quotations in this chapter are from "Circus Diary—Part II" unless otherwise identified.

129 **"Faced with the search for structure, sit back and sift, shuffle and stack"**: Cheney, *Writing Creative Nonfiction*, 140. Henri drew a line alongside this paragraph.

131 **Rodleigh stayed to do the rigging while Jennie took Henri to the railway station**: Stevens, "What a Friend We Had in Henri," 16–17.

Chapter 21

132 **"I sense that Franz still has some problems with my enthusiasm for the circus"**: All Nouwen quotations in this chapter are from "Circus Diary—Part II" unless otherwise identified.

133 **The apartment on the third floor**: Henri wrote several books during various stays with Franz and Reny, including *Our Greatest Gift*.

136 **"Listen to everyone"**: Henri underlined this passage in Cheney, *Writing Creative Nonfiction*, 127.

137 **After affectionate farewells in the early morning**: Stevens, "What a Friend We Had in Henri," 18.

Chapter 22

139 **"how individualistic and elitist my own spirituality had been"** . . . **"a spirituality for introspective persons"**: Quotations from Henri Nouwen, "Foreword," in Gustavo Gutierrez, *We Drink from Our Own Wells: The Spiritual Journey of a People* (Maryknoll, NY: Orbis Books, 1984), xvi.

140 **"I've seen very clearly that all together form one body, as a whole"**: Interview with Jan van den Bosch, in film *Henri Nouwen: The Passion of a Wounded Healer*, Christian Catalyst Collection, EO Television, available on Amazon Prime (as of January 2021).

140 **Less than two weeks after Henri lurched away in his camper van**: This account of Henri's letter to Rodleigh in June 1992 draws on Stevens, "What a Friend We Had in Henri," 19.

140 **he wrote to John Dear**: Dear, *The Road to Peace*, xxiv.

140 **At the end of November, Henri again wrote to Rodleigh:** Stevens, "What a Friend We Had in Henri," 19.

141 **He could easily imagine using three movements:** This draft outline is in Henri's 1992 unpublished notebook held in the Nouwen Archives. All quotations in this chapter from the outline come from this notebook.

142 **"I don't want to write just another book":** Nouwen, interview in English in the unedited footage for the film *Angels Over the Net*. A condensed version of this quotation is also in the final English version of the film.

143 **"Why should I write about a trapeze act?":** Nouwen, "Circus Diary—Part II," 8.

Chapter 23

144 **The painting illustrated a story Jesus had told:** Jesus's parable of the Prodigal Son is found in the New Testament of the Bible, Luke 15:11–32.

145 **So he meditated on Rembrandt's painting:** Nouwen, *The Return of the Prodigal Son*, 3–15, 19.

145 **In England, his friend Bart Gavigan urged Henry to see himself also in the older son:** Nouwen, *The Return of the Prodigal Son*, 18.

146 **As he began to find some peace in his own body:** Nouwen, *The Return of the Prodigal Son*, 19–20.

146 **When the book was done, he tried a few titles:** These unfortunate titles for Henri's Prodigal Son book are found in his handwriting on the title page of Draft 4 of his manuscript, held in the Nouwen Archives. Gabrielle Earnshaw in *Henri Nouwen and the Return of the Prodigal Son* provides many more details about the writing of Henri's most famous book.

147 **"They were trying to do something new":** Nouwen, "The Flying Rodleighs—The Circus," 8–9.

Chapter 24

149 **"When I saw the Flying Rodleighs for the first time":** Nouwen, "Letter to Bart Gavigan, December 2, 1994," held in the Nouwen Archives.

150 **"To me it's very fascinating that this art":** Nouwen, interview with Jan van den Bosch, in his film *Henri Nouwen: The Passion of a Wounded Healer*.

150 **Henri's friend Frank Hamilton read Henri's 1992 journal:** This

account of Frank Hamilton offering to join Henri in his June 1993 visit to the Flying Rodleighs draws on "Interview with Frank Hamilton," Henri Nouwen Oral History Project, interview by Sue Mosteller, November 1, 2005, transcript page 35. The audio interview and transcript are held in the Nouwen Archives.

151 **Ron sipped his coffee and took his time answering:** Personal email from Ron P. van den Bosch, November 2020.

151 **"I came to know the trapeze life from within":** Nouwen, interview in English in the unedited footage for the film *Angels Over the Net*. Everything in the quotation except the first sentence is also in the final English version of the film.

152 **Henri arrived with Frank in June 1993:** Stevens, "What a Friend We Had in Henri," 19–22.

152 **"What do you think?" Henri asked his friends earnestly:** Adapted from "Interview with Frank Hamilton" by Sue Mosteller, Henri Nouwen Oral History Project, November 1, 2005.

153 **Jennie's lunch the next day:** Stevens, "What a Friend We Had in Henri," 22.

153 **One afternoon, Henri urged Ron to take a photo:** Stevens, "What a Friend We Had in Henri," 22.

Chapter 25

155 **The highlight of the 1993 visit was on June 6:** Nouwen, unpublished handwritten notes in "June 6th '93" entry in his notebook "Flying Rodleighs Technical Description of the Trapeze Act Circus Barum 1992," Nouwen Archives.

156 **Rodleigh enjoyed seeing Henri on the platform:** Stevens, "What a Friend We Had in Henri," 22.

158 **"I really like them, Henri":** Adapted from "Interview with Frank Hamilton," by Sue Mosteller.

158 **"The act is like a Russian icon":** The direct quotations in italics in this scene of brainstorming about Henri's book come from Henri's unpublished handwritten entries titled "Notes by Frank" in a notebook started in 1992 and still being used in 1993, titled on the front cover "Circus Barum, Diary, Notes." This notebook is held in the Nouwen Archives. Henri's notes sometimes identify Ron or Frank as the speaker. Frank Hamilton has confirmed

that my reconstruction of their conversation from Henri's notes accurately depicts what he remembers. In his initial comment, Frank may have been referring to Henri's book about icons, *Behold the Beauty of the Lord: Praying with Icons* (South Bend, IN: Ave Maria Press, 1987).

Chapter 26

160 **Rodleigh did not see Henri again until a brief visit in November 1993:** Stevens, "What a Friend We Had in Henri," 24–25.

160 **When Henri sent him a copy of *Our Greatest Gift*:** Stevens, "What a Friend We Had in Henri," 27.

160 **It was not that he had no religious background:** Henri's unpublished transcript "Interviews with Karlene Stevens and Rodleigh Stevens, November 1991," held in the Nouwen Archives.

161 **"One day, I was sitting with Rodleigh, the leader of the troupe, in his caravan, talking about flying":** Nouwen, *Our Greatest Gift*, 67.

Chapter 27

163 **"I love these trapeze artists a lot!":** On May 3, 1994, at the Dialogue '94: A Call to Partnership conference in Milwaukee, Wisconsin, Henri received the COMISS Medallion (Coalition On Ministry In Specialized Setting), presented to a person who has made an outstanding contribution internationally to the field of pastoral care, counseling, and education. The presentation and his lively talk can be viewed on YouTube: www.youtube.com/watch?v=9hHB0Ph6eKc.

165 **By 1994, AIDS had become the leading cause of death:** For a sense of how the AIDS pandemic grew, see https://www.hiv.gov/hiv-basics/overview/history/hiv-and-aids-timeline. Henri had been grieving the loss of friends, connecting with and supporting people in the AIDS networks since the beginning of the pandemic. See Henri J. M. Nouwen, *Love, Henri: Letters on the Spiritual Life*, ed. Gabrielle Earnshaw (New York: Convergent Books, 2016), 112–13.

165 **"I am really very grateful for being here this whole week":** All quotations of Henri from his talk at the 1994 conference come from the audio recording Henri Nouwen, "As I Have Done So You Are Called to Do," July 26, 1994, at the 1994 Seventh National Catholic HIV/AIDS Min-

istry Conference in Chicago. This audio recording is held in the Nouwen Archives. An abbreviated written version was published as Henri Nouwen, "Our Story, Our Wisdom," in *The Road to Peace*, ed. Dear, 175–83.

Chapter 28

170 **All his life, his father has liked:** Henri often spoke of his father's particular appreciation for intelligent people, books, and analysis.

171 **"One of the parts of the act that deeply moves me":** Nouwen, letter to Bart Gavigan, December 2, 1994.

172 **By the summer of 1994, Henri decided:** This account of preparing for and making the *Angels Over the Net* film draws on Stevens, "What a Friend We Had in Henri," 28–33.

172 **"The Flying Rodleighs are a trapeze group":** Nouwen, letter to Bart Gavigan, December 2, 1994.

172 **Henri's friend Jan interviewed him for the film:** All quotations of Jan van den Bosch and Henri come from the interview in English in the unedited footage for the film *Angels Over the Net*. About a quarter of the quotation here is also included in the final English version of the film.

174 **"We all want to make triples and doubles and layouts and double doubles":** Nouwen, interview in English in the unedited footage for the film *Angels Over the Net*. This quotation is included in the final English version of the film.

174 **"Now I live and work with people with mental handicaps":** Nouwen, interview in English in the unedited footage for the film *Angels Over the Net*. Everything quoted here is also found in the final English version of the film. For clarity, I have put what Henri says about the Rodleighs after what he says about his L'Arche community.

Chapter 29

177 **His friends Sue Mosteller and Kathy Bruner came with him:** Sue Mosteller told me about how anxious Henri was about this second conference. The interpretive dance at the 1995 AIDS conference and Henri's response were described to me by Henri's and my friend Kathy Bruner.

178 **This time Henri boldly titled his talk "Befriending Death":** Henri Nouwen, "Befriending Death," Eighth National Catholic HIV/AIDS Min-

istry Conference, July 1995, in Chicago. A written version of the talk was published by the National Catholic AIDS Network. An audio recording and a copy of the published text of the talk are held in the Nouwen Archives. All further quotations in this chapter are from Nouwen, "Befriending Death," unless otherwise identified.

180 **"When I met the Rodleighs and I saw their work":** Nouwen, unedited footage for the film *Angels Over the Net*. This quotation is included in the final English version of the film.

Chapter 30

183 **After admiring the cover's bright detail:** As Henri began his sabbatical, he was especially delighted with his beautiful hardcover journals. I remember him holding up the bright covers for us to admire at the beginning of his 1995–96 sabbatical.

183 **"Oakville, Ontario, Saturday, September 2, 1995":** "Saturday September 2, 1995" entry in Nouwen, handwritten 1995–96 sabbatical journals. A condensed version of this passage is also in Nouwen, *Sabbatical Journey*, 3.

184 **"I have written many essays, reflections, and meditations":** "Friday September 8, 1995" entry in Nouwen, handwritten 1995–96 sabbatical journals. This passage is also in Nouwen, *Sabbatical Journey*, 10–11.

184 **in early December, while staying with friends in Massachusetts:** "Sunday December 3, 1995" entry in Nouwen, handwritten 1995–96 sabbatical journals.

Chapter 31

186 **A snowstorm was closing in:** "Dec 14–17, 1995" entries in Nouwen, handwritten 1995–96 sabbatical journals. Parts are edited and included in Nouwen, *Sabbatical Journey*, 65–69.

187 **Joan was a gifted musician:** Someone who spent time with Henri and Joan told me that together they were "like peas in a pod." For more information about Joan Kroc's wide-ranging interests, including her career as a pianist, see Lisa Napoli's *Ray & Joan: The Man Who Made the McDonald's Fortune and the Woman Who Gave It All Away* (New York: Dutton Penguin Random House, 2016). Joan's comments about and to children in 1998 can be seen

here: https://www.youtube.com/watch?v=VgLbicSvJxY. In the mid-1980s, Joan established the Kroc Institute for International Peace Studies at the University of Notre Dame (see https://kroc.nd.edu/), and in 2000 began the Joan B. Kroc School of Peace Studies at the University of San Diego (see https://www.sandiego.edu/peace/). For an overview of her contributions to her community and the world, see the 2004 video made when Joan B. Kroc was inducted into the San Diego Women's Hall of Fame: https://www.youtube.com/watch?v=qgA0AMimHBI.

187 **"My experience is that rich people are also poor, but in other ways":** Henri J. M. Nouwen, *Spirituality of Fundraising* (Nashville: Upper Room Books, 2011), 18.

189 **"Unconditional love is love without conditions, without strings attached":** "A Reflection on Unconditional Love for Joan Kroc," in Nouwen, *Love, Henri*, 332.

189 **"But when you see these trapeze artists, it becomes a symbol":** Nouwen, "The Flying Rodleighs—The Circus," 26.

189 **"This unconditional love is the love that Jesus calls us to 'love your enemies'":** Nouwen, *Love, Henri*, 332–33.

190 **"I was fascinated by their dedication, by their discipline":** Nouwen, "The Flying Rodleighs—The Circus," 26.

191 **"It is not a sentimental, all approving, and always agreeing love":** Nouwen, *Love, Henri*, 334.

Chapter 32

192 **"I was so bombarded":** "Friday October 20, 1995" entry in Nouwen, handwritten 1995–96 sabbatical journals. An edited condensed version of this passage is also in Nouwen, *Sabbatical Journey*, 40–41.

193 **"Spectacular as it was, nothing":** "Thursday December 28, 1995" entry in Nouwen, handwritten 1995–96 sabbatical journals. A rephrased version of this passage is also in Nouwen, *Sabbatical Journey*, 74–75.

193 **A few days later, Henri was overjoyed:** "Sunday January 7, 1996" entry in Nouwen, handwritten 1995–96 sabbatical journals. An edited version of this passage is also in Nouwen, *Sabbatical Journey*, 82–83.

194 **Rodleigh noted with concern how exhausted Henri looked:** This

account of Rodleigh reflecting on their friendship with Henri draws on Stevens, "What a Friend We Had in Henri," 37, 41–42.

196 **"As I reflected on this short visit":** "Sunday January 7, 1996" entry in Nouwen, handwritten 1995–96 sabbatical journals. An edited version of this passage is also in Nouwen, *Sabbatical Journey*, 83.

Chapter 33

197 **Because the heating system did not work, they huddled by the open fire:** "Wednesday January 24, 1996" entry in Nouwen, handwritten 1995–96 sabbatical journals. This passage is also in Nouwen, *Sabbatical Journey*, 94.

198 **his "secret journal":** Passages from his 1987–88 breakdown are quoted from his original handwritten 1987–88 journals. These are held in the Nouwen Archives. Many passages from these journals were edited and included in *The Inner Voice of Love*.

198 **"a certain fear about working on the manuscript":** "Friday January 26, 1996" entry in Nouwen, handwritten 1995–96 sabbatical journals. This passage is also in Nouwen, *Sabbatical Journey*, 94.

198 **"Trust, trust that God will give you that all-fulfilling love":** "Sunday Jan 17" entry in Nouwen, handwritten 1987–88 journals.

198 **"The Flying Rodleighs teach me something about being in the body":** Nouwen, interview in the unedited footage for the film *Angels Over the Net*.

199 **his hitchhiking friend Charles:** Nouwen, "We Shall Overcome," 77.

199 **"I said to myself, 'Yes, yes, I belong; these are my people'":** Nouwen, *Our Greatest Gift*, 25.

199 **Friends remembered his desperate late-night phone calls or visits:** See the accounts by Parker Palmer and Yushi Nomura quoted in Ford, *Wounded Prophet*, 37–38.

200 **"Until now my whole life has been centered around the word":** "Thursday March 20, 1986" journal entry published in Henri J. M. Nouwen, "To Meet the Body Is to Meet the Word," *New Oxford Review* 54, no. 3 (April 1987): 3–4. This quotation was not included in Henri's 1985–86 journal selections published as Nouwen, *The Road to Daybreak*.

200 **"My closeness to him and to his body":** Nouwen, *Adam*, 49.

201 **"Next I want to talk about the body"**: Nouwen, "As I Have Done So You Are Called to Do."

201 **"When I saw the Rodleighs for the first time I said I missed my vocation"**: Nouwen, interview in English in the unedited footage for the film *Angels Over the Net*. This quotation is included in the final English version of the film.

202 **"And then there was the intimacy thing"**: Nouwen, "The Flying Rodleighs—The Circus," 27–28.

202 **"The Flying Rodleighs express"**: Nouwen, letter to Bart Gavigan, December 2, 1994.

203 **"Every human being lives a sexual life"**: Ford, *Lonely Mystic*, 58.

203 **Early in 1996, he amused some of his New York editors**: As recounted by one of the editors who was present.

Chapter 34

204 **Henri's secretary phoned him in New Jersey**: "Monday February 12, 1996" entry in Nouwen, handwritten 1995–96 sabbatical journals.

204 **"Living together with Adam at L'Arche Daybreak"**: "Wednesday February 12, 1996" entry in Nouwen, handwritten 1995–96 sabbatical journals. These passages are also in Nouwen, *Sabbatical Journey*, 103.

205 **"Seeing Adam's body in the casket touched me deeply"**: "Monday February 14, 1996" entry in Nouwen, handwritten 1995–96 sabbatical journals. A version of this passage is also in Nouwen, *Sabbatical Journey*, 107.

205 **"Adam gave me a sense of belonging"**: Nouwen, *Adam*, 126–27.

206 **"It became a quite remarkable evening"**: "March 6, 1996" entry in Nouwen, handwritten 1995–96 sabbatical journals. An edited version of this passage is in Nouwen, *Sabbatical Journey*, 121–22.

Chapter 35

208 **"What I most hope is to learn"**: "Friday May 17, 1996" entry in Nouwen, handwritten 1995–96 sabbatical journals. This passage is also in Nouwen, *Sabbatical Journey*, 167.

208 **"Although I had come to Santa Fe"**: "Sunday May 19, 1996" entry in

Nouwen, handwritten 1995–96 sabbatical journals. An edited version of this passage is also in Nouwen, *Sabbatical Journey*, 168.

210 **In the middle of the week, Joan Kroc's plane:** Henri's lunch with Joan is recorded on "Wednesday May 22, 1996," while his reflections on O'Keeffe are from his "Monday May 20, 1996" entry in Nouwen, handwritten 1995–96 sabbatical journals.

Chapter 36

211 **He prefers not to travel alone:** Henri writes about this in *Here and Now*, 85–86.

211 **"I hadn't expected that I would be so moved":** "Tuesday July 9, 1996" entry in Nouwen, handwritten 1995–96 sabbatical journals. This passage is also in Nouwen, *Sabbatical Journey*, 194–95.

212 **Rodleigh watched Henri:** Stevens, "What a Friend We Had in Henri," 39. The catcher who held Henri on that day was John Vokes, who had replaced Joe. To avoid adding another new name to the story, I have called that catcher by the name of the other catcher, Henri's friend Jon Griggs, who was still with the troupe.

212 **"At the end of the practice session":** "Wednesday July 10, 1996" entry in Nouwen, handwritten 1995–96 sabbatical journals. A slightly edited version of this passage is also in Nouwen, *Sabbatical Journey*, 195–96.

213 **"It was a warm and heartfelt good-bye":** "Thursday July 11, 1996" entry in Nouwen, handwritten 1995–96 sabbatical journals.

Chapter 37

215 **Henri pulled out the final journals he had acquired for his sabbatical:** Henri's journals from his sabbatical year are held in the Nouwen Archives; the cover art is identified by the publishers of the blank journals in printed notes inside the back cover. Online, the Metropolitan Museum of Art describes the images on the front of Henri's last two journals: "On the left side of the coffin box there is an architectural facade with a small doorway in the center at the bottom. This is the equivalent of the Old Kingdom false door, which allowed the spirit of the deceased to move between the land of the dead and the land of the living. In this case, it is painted to

resemble two wooden door leaves secured with two door bolts. Above the door are two eyes that look forth into the land of the living." See "Coffin of Khnumnakht," the Met, https://www.metmuseum.org/art/collection /search/544326.

216 **"I know now that I have to speak from eternity into time":** Nouwen, *The Return of the Prodigal Son*, 15.

216 **some friends had urged him to come out as a gay man:** See *The Essential Henri Nouwen*, ed. Robert A. Jonas (Boulder, CO: Shambhala Publications, 2009), xxviii–xl, and Ford, *Wounded Prophet*, 193–94.

216 **Aware that his sexual orientation could be revealed without his consent, Henri was often uneasy:** This was told to me by Henri's friends.

216 **"unresolvable struggle" and "My sexuality will remain":** From July 1996 letters, quoted by his archivist Gabrielle Earnshaw in *Love, Henri*, xv.

216 **"about the anxiety that had been plaguing me":** "Saturday May 4, 1996" in Nouwen, handwritten 1995–96 sabbatical journals—slightly rephrased in *Sabbatical Journey*, 207.

217 **he automatically began to gnaw on his fingernails:** The Gavigans write, "he himself was spectacularly ill at ease in his body. You had only to watch the way he walked or glance at those bitten-to-the-quick fingernails to recognize the inner battle"; in "Collision and Paradox," *Befriending Life*, 55.

217 **"I often wonder how I would survive emotionally":** "Wednesday July 31, 1996" entry in Nouwen, handwritten 1995–96 sabbatical journals.

217 **"Trapeze was my secret door":** These two sentences about the trapeze are written by Henri and quoted in Jim Smith's unpublished March 25, 1996, letter to Henri Nouwen. Smith's letter is held in the Nouwen Archives, and used with permission from Jim Smith. Smith's letter highlights and repeats these two sentences as part of his response to Henri.

Chapter 38

218 **"She welcomed me warmly and took me right away to a restaurant":** "Fri August 16, 1996" entry in Nouwen, handwritten 1995–96 sabbatical journals.

219 **"Let's go to the races in Del Mar," Joan said:** "Sat August 17, 1996" entry in Nouwen, handwritten 1995–96 sabbatical journals. An abbreviated version is also in Nouwen, *Sabbatical Journey*, 214–15.

220 **For almost forty years, he had been catching God:** Nouwen was ordained a Catholic priest for the Archdiocese of Utrecht on July 21, 1957.

220 **She poured Henri another glass of the 1973 Rothschild wine:** In his handwritten journal, Henri describes their meal: *At 7pm Joan and I had a very nice Mexican dinner with Enchiladas and Rice—with a bottle of Red Wine such as I have never tasted before. Rothschild 1973! Joan said: "It goes down like velvet, don't you think? Ray bought it twenty years ago. It says you have to drink it before the year 2000."* "Sat August 17, 1996" entry in Nouwen, handwritten 1995–96 sabbatical journals. I have invented the conversation over dinner in which Joan suggests to Henri that he is a catcher of God. I owe this insight to Geoffrey Whitney-Brown.

221 **"'strange as it may sound, we can become like God for others'":** Nouwen, *Love, Henri*, 333. After the August 1996 weekend with Joan, Henri wrote, "It feels that Joan and I are more relaxed with one another and are indeed becoming friends. A friendship that allows us to speak openly and directly about our real concerns. The great luxury surrounding me seemed less distracting. I felt like our time together had been fruitful and spiritually valuable." "18 August, 1996" entry in Nouwen, handwritten 1995–96 sabbatical journals. Seven years later, as Joan Kroc was dying of cancer, "there was little else she could do but thumb through the leather-bound Bible given her by the late Father Henri Nouwen": Napoli, *Ray & Joan*, 12.

221 **"That love sends us out to serve joyously":** In a letter for her granddaughter Amanda's twenty-first birthday, Joan wrote, "I want you to believe that a life of service is a happy one to lead. Serve others joyously. . . ." A video of Amanda reading Joan's letter aloud can be found at: https://www.youtube.com/watch?v=BQ8znSUilLc.

Chapter 39

222 **"Life is a precarious balance":** From an interview by Jan van den Bosch, in his film *Henri Nouwen: The Passion of a Wounded Healer*.

222 **"I feel quite anxious interiorly":** "Saturday May 4, 1996" entry in

Nouwen, handwritten 1995–96 sabbatical journals. An edited version of this passage is also in Nouwen, *Sabbatical Journey*, 160.

223 **drifting from place to place like a hungry ghost:** Henri wrote about his fascination with the Tibetan Buddhist concept of the hungry ghost in his "6 Feb 1996" entry in Nouwen, handwritten 1995–96 sabbatical journals, then in his "7 Feb 1996" entry he noted with self-aware humor that all day he felt like a hungry ghost. See also Nouwen, *Sabbatical Journey*, 99–100.

223 **Henri remembers how his embarrassment:** "Wednesday July 10, 1996" entry in Nouwen, handwritten 1995–96 sabbatical journals. Rodleigh Stevens also describes this scene in Stevens, "What a Friend We Had in Henri," 22–23.

225 **"When we radically claim God's unconditional love for us, we can forgive":** Nouwen, *Love, Henri*, 333.

225 **"I sometimes have thought, how would it be":** Nouwen, "As I Have Done So You Are Called to Do." See also Nouwen, *Here and Now*, 60–61.

225 **"through the eyes of God":** Nouwen, *The Return of the Prodigal Son*, 15, quoted in Chapter 37.

225 **"A trick is not complete unless":** Henri J. M. Nouwen, "Technicalities of Trapeze Movements: I. the Full-Twisting Double Lay-Out by Rodleigh," May 1992, 9. This typed transcript of Henri's unpublished handwritten notebook is held in the Nouwen Archives.

225 **"The Rodleighs are saying to me indirectly, don't be afraid to fly a little":** Nouwen, interview in English in the unedited footage for the film *Angels Over the Net*. This quotation is also found in the final English version of the film.

226 **He feels like he has been rising:** See Chapter 2 notes: "the trapeze became a dream for me. To be a trapeze artist symbolized for me the realization of the human desire for self-transcendence–rising above oneself, glimpsing the heart of things." The final sentence of the last book published in Henri's lifetime reads: "Together when we drink that cup as Jesus drank it we are transformed into the one body of the living Christ, always dying and always rising for the salvation of the world." Nouwen, *Can You Drink the Cup?* (Notre Dame, IN: Ave Maria Press, 1996), 111.

Epilogue

227 **"As the three flyers swung away from the pedestal board":** Nouwen, "Chapter I," 9–10.

227 **Henri didn't die:** An account of Henri's last days in the hospital can be found in Nathan Ball's afterword to *Sabbatical Journey,* 223–26. See also Ford, *Wounded Prophet,* 200–207. Ball later wrote, "Henri's heart attack was indeed a gift that helped him to make a passage. . . . He had many struggles and shared them openly with his friends and through his numerous writings. But this I know: Henri died at peace with himself, his family, his own faith community of L'Arche, his friends, his vocation as a priest, and the God whose everlasting love had been Henri's beacon for sixty-four years." Nouwen, *Sabbatical Journey,* 226. Henri ended *The Inner Voice of Love,* which he was working on during his sabbatical and which arrived in bookstores the day of his Canadian funeral, with the words: "I have heard the inner voice of love, deeper and stronger than ever. I want to keep trusting in that voice and be led by it beyond the boundaries of my short life, to where God is all in all" (118).

228 **News of Henri's death reached the Flying Rodleighs:** Stevens, "What a Friend We Had in Henri," 1.

229 **During the long week as we waited for Henri's return:** Details about his two caskets are my own memories as a member of the Daybreak community. At the time, I was working in the Daybreak woodworking shop. I asked community members to create art for Henri, then I painted the community members' images onto the lid of Henri's casket: see Whitney-Brown, "Henri at Daybreak." For a photo and short description, see my Daybreak blog post "The Painted Doors of the Dayspring Chapel," September 1, 2019, https://larchedaybreak.com/the-painted-doors-of-the-dayspring-chapel%EF%BB%BF-by-carrie-whitney-brown/.

229 **Henri's body was buried twice:** Henri's remains were moved to St. John's Anglican Church in November 2010. Details about this second burial were provided by Sue Mosteller. See also Michael Swan, "Famous Catholic Author Nouwen Moved to Anglican Cemetery," *Catholic Register,* November 25, 2010, https://www.catholicregister.org/item/9400-famous-catholic-author-nouwen-moved-to-anglican-cemetery.

230 **"I suddenly realized that's what life is all about":** Transcribed from Henri's talk after receiving the COMISS Medallion in May 1994.

CREDITS AND PERMISSIONS